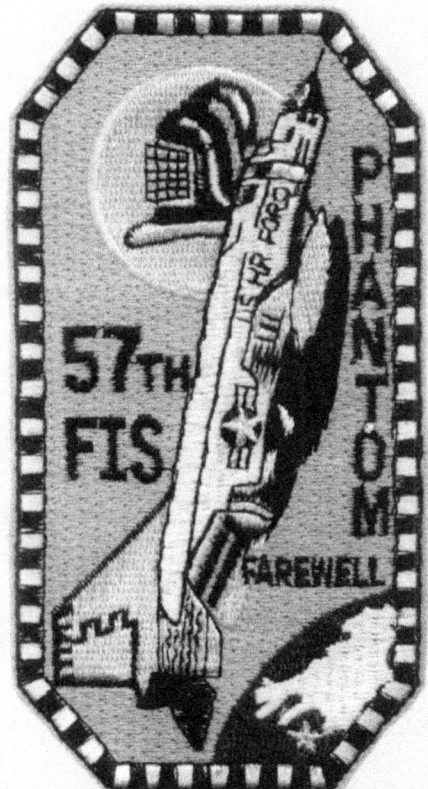

F-4 Phantom II Society

Turner Publishing Company

Turner Publishing Company
412 Broadway • P.O. Box 3101
Paducah, KY 42002-3101
(270) 443-0121

Turner Publishing Company Staff:
Editor: Randy Baumgardner
Designer: Heather R. Warren

Copyright © 2001
Turner Publishing Company
ISBN 978-1-63026-942-5

Library of Congress
Control No: 2001-087260

This book was created using available materials. The publisher regrets that it cannot assume liability for errors or omissions. This publication or any part thereof may not be reproduced without the written consent of the author and publisher.

Photo Cover: The 117TRW twentieth anniversary RF-4C Phantom, May 1990. This Phantom, 65-854 was the 117TRW Wing Commanders Aircraft, Gen. Jim Brown, and sports the additional markings denoted that the unit has twenty years in the Phantom. (Courtesy of Don Spering/AIR)

Photo previous page: RF4C-Nevada Air National Guard - The High Rollers. (Courtesy of R.G. Langley)

Final Line-up RF4C's of the Nevada Air National Guard. Courtesy of R.G. Langley

Table of Contents

Introduction 8
Publisher's Message 9
History of the F-4 Phantom II, by Pat Martin 10
Special Stories of the F-4 Phantom II 28
Photo Gallery 40
Biographies of the F-4 Phantom II Society 78
Index 95

F-4C's, 63-553/432/64-827, fly echelon for the camera. The distinctive blue and white tail band and stars are the colors of the 196 TFS/163 TFG, based at March AFB, CA. September 1985. Courtesy of Don Spering/AIR.

F-4E of the 34 TFS 388 TFW refueling from a KC-135A returning from combat sortie in September 1969. Photo courtesy of A. Bruder.

Introduction

For over a year members of the Phantom Society and Turner Publishing Company have been working on this Phantom Society book. The society was formed by enthusiasts interested in the study and preservation of the F-4 Phantom. This large fighter aircraft, built by McDonnell Aircraft Corporation and powered by General Electric J79 engines, proved to be a winner by all standards. The aircraft has made its place in history, through several conflicts and by greatly contributing to the balance of power during the Cold War.

The Phantom was, and still is, used as a term of measurement in fighter talk. As this was written, some forty-two years after first flying, the Phantom is still receiving upgrades as a front fighter-bomber in several countries. This ensures it will be some time before fuel is no longer converted into noise, smoke and forward motion by the Phantom. But the day will come when the Phantom will no longer take the skies in military service. Then it will only be seen by the public as an exotic flying warbird and perhaps on the grounds of a museum where it joins other icons of the past.

With this book the Phantom Society honors all those who have manufactured, worked, maintained, and flew the F-4. To those fortunate enough to have the Phantom in their past, even if only to see it fly, reminisce; to those in the future who will never see the Phantom fly, you missed the show.

Enjoy!

Pat Martin, Editor
Smoke Trails

Spring 1966, F-4B, VF-114 Bond 152227. USS Kitty Hawk CVA-63. Individual at right is deceased. Courtesy of Val Valentine.

Publisher's Message

Dave Turner - President, Turner Publishing Company

It has been an honor working with the F–4 Phantom II Society on this historical volume on one of the finest aircraft every built. Her length of service and world–wide application are a tribute to her design, a heavy-duty fighter built for the ages.

The stories, biographies and photos within these pages are from both the military and civilian sector. This unique blend of individuals include those who have flown this powerful machine, but also aviation photographers and military brats, and some who simply have a fascination for the F–4. All together, it is this delicate mix that makes the F–4 Phantom II Society so special.

I must give a very special "thank you" to Pat Martin, F–4 Society Historian and editor of SmokeTrails, who helped research, write and proof this outstanding volume. I would also like to thank Cmdrs. Jan Jacobs and Steve Eisner, whose leadership in the F–4 Phantom "Phanclub" are well known, and without whose help this book could not have surfaced.

It is with great pleasure that I present, to all the "Phantom Phaithful", this tribute to the F–4 Phantom. May it give you fond memories for years to come.

Sincerely yours,

Dave Turner
President

History of the F-4 Phantom II

MCAS Beaufort was a major base for USMC Phantoms. F-4J Phantom from VMFA-451 awaits use at Beaufort in June 1972. Photo courtesy of Frank MacSorely.

The following is a brief narrative history of the McDonnell Phantom II. Volumes have been written on this most outstanding aircraft. The first Phantom took to the air in 1958, only thirteen years after the Second World War ended. The need for a longer range and more powerful naval fighter brought forward the design of the F4H-1, later known as the F-4A and more famously or infamously, depending on your country of origin, the Phantom II. The Phantom's longevity became all the more amazing when at the turn of the century, 42 years later, hundreds were still flying with ever greater increased abilities. What made the Phantom? Initially it was the great power provided by a pair of General Electric J79 engines and the APQ-50 radar with 24 inch dish, coupled with an airframe that could carry a large weapon load over greater distances, all in great excess of aircraft it replaced.

THE PHANTOM

For decades aviation enthusiasts have been enthralled with the sound and sight of the aircraft known simply as, the Phantom. Only eight years after the end of the Second World War, the US Navy sent out its request for proposals for what would eventually become a fifteen-ton machine that would awe both friend and foe alike. In course, this would decisively alter at least one conflict.

The F-4 Phantom was not the first aircraft to use the name "Phantom". The previous Phantom was also a McDonnell product. It was a small, twin-jet engine, straight wing fighter that first flew in 1945. The complete history could have been written within five and a half years when the last of the 60 production examples was retired. The type later led to the development of the successful Banshee, of which 892 were built. The immediate predecessor of the Phantom II, also from McDonnell, was the less than successful F3H Demon. The Demon was plagued with cost over-runs and an extended development period. In a large degree, this was due to the single unreliable power plant. If the Phantom II was considered by some to be "double-ugly", then the Demon must have been considered to be just "ugly".

In October 1954, the US Navy gave McDonnell a letter of intent for two prototype aircraft to be known as the YF4H-1. The original intent was thought to be aimed more towards the all-weather attack role. This was changed to all-weather fighter in May 1955 and the two prototypes would be designated as XF4H-1. Two months later a further contract was awarded for five pre-production aircraft. McDonnell was issued a further contract in December 1956, for 16 production F4H-1.

The aircraft was to be a twin-seat, twin-engine, Mach-2, carrier capable, all-weather fighter. The idea of a twin-seat fighter was not entirely new to the US Navy, as it had operated specialized night-fighter types such as the Grumman Tigercat and Douglas Skyknight. The aircraft was to be powered by a pair of J79 engines. The planned 20mm cannon installation was canceled in favor of a quartet of Sparrow missiles; semi-submerged beneath the fuselage, plus five pylons for stores. This would make the Phantom the first missile-only armed naval jet

The IAI Kurnass 2000 or Super Phantom prototype 4X-JPA taxies out for an air display at the 1987 Paris air show. Photo Hans Schroder Via Martin slides.

The prototype F4H-1 flying with an escorting RF-101 Voodoo over the Californian desert. The nose structure was much smaller on the prototype than the F-4B model onwards. Photo via Phantom Society.

fighter. The missile-verse-gun debate had not yet been settled, as painful lessons had yet to be learned.

The first prototype lifted off from Lambert Field, St. Louis, on May 27, 1958, at the hands of Robert C. Little. The first flight was not exactly smooth, with the nose gear failing to fully retract. The fault was traced to the hydraulic system. The nose gear problem persisted into the second flight. Mach one was exceeded on the third flight with the co-operation of the nose gear!

The competition for production contracts would be against the established, but greatly improved Crusader, in the form of unconventional Chance Vought F8U-3 Crusader III. Many historians still think this aircraft would have had a great future. Following US Navy evaluation, the Phantom II won a further contract for 24 airframes. All 45 pre-production and production aircraft were designated F4H-1F due to the use of the J79-GE-2 engines. Later early models used the J79-GE-8.

Development work continued with improvements and adjustments occurring. One very noticeable feature was the redesign of the canopy area to vacillate improved rear cockpit visibility. This redesign allowed the newer APQ-72 radar with its 32 inch dish to increase efficiency. A boundary-layer control system for compressed air blown over the forward and aft flap sections was incorporated.

The USAF evaluated the Phantom II as a long range interceptor for Air Defense Command. Although the Phantom II had the ability to carry heavier loads over greater distances than current ADC types, the missile system was not designed with the same intent. The Phantom II was seen as having great potential as a tactical fighter and reconnaissance platform. This cumulated with a March 1962 contract for a single F-110A from the USAF. Two months later, this was expanded with contracts for two YRF-110A for the reconnaissance role.

In 1962, all three services adopted a common aircraft designation system. The F4H became the F-4. For the US Navy, the J79-GE-2 equipped aircraft became F-4A and those with the production intended J79-GE-8 became the F-4B. The USAF F-110A became the F-4C and the FR-110A, the RF-4C. All other variants were designated as the F-4, as they came post 1962.

With the heating up of the Cold War the future of the fighter from St. Louis was assured. A total of 5,195 Phantoms were built, including 127 under license. The Phantom was exported to 11 nations and built in the following major variants—

XF4H-1

Two prototypes, very small nose profile.

F-4A   F4H-1F

Forty-five pre-production aircraft. Some brought up to F-4B standards.

F-4B   F4H-1

Production run of 649 aircraft. This became the standard carrier tactical strike fighter, as used by the US Navy and USMC. The aircraft saw extensive use in Southeast Asia. Its replacement, another Phantom, the F-4J. Many were modified in conversion programs; 29 were loaned to the USAF to assist transition prior to USAF deliveries of the F-4C, twelve were temporarily modified to F-4G with AN/ASW-21 two-way data link systems (unrelated to the later Wild Weasel F-4G), three modified to YF-4J standard, over 40 were converted to drone configured QF-4B, one, possibly three became electronic configured EF-4B and 228 rebuilt as F-4N.

RF-4B

A total of 46 RF-4B were manufactured during production of other versions as a tactical reconnaissance platform for the USMC, first flying in March 1965. The fleet received various upgrades to the airframe and systems until withdrawn from use in late 1990. The RF-4B and subsequent RF Phantoms were equipped with smaller nose mounted ground mapping radar instead of the air-to-air system, making room for reconnaissance systems. Built in two basic sub models. Based on the F-4B with thin wings and skinny tires. The second batch was up to F-4J standards, except engines, but with thicker tires and wings. Survivors changed to J79-GE-10B smokeless engines with longer burner cans.

F-4C

Although similar to the USN and USMC F-4B, the F-4C had numerous changes within to suit USAF requirements. The rear cockpit had controls, which differed from the US Navy standard of using a RIO. The probe and drogue aerial refueling system was replaced by the USAF receptacle and boom system placed behind the cockpit, as per all USAF versions. Had the thicker tires and wings. The radar, avionics, inertial navigation and weapons fit were all tailored for the USAF. This model of the Phantom became the premiere tactical fighter in the USAF inventory with an eventual 583 built. The F-4C also served in the defense suppression role until the introduction of the F-4G Wild Weasel, with up to 36 examples converted. After gradual replacement in the fighter and tactical roles by the F-4D and F-4E, the F-4C went on to serve with the Air Force Reserve and Air National Guard units. Spain was the only foreign recipient of the F-4C.

RF-4C

Production of the RF-4C was initially based on the F-4C, and equipped with weapons systems and a smaller radar. Various intelligence gathering systems were used over the years, including cameras and radar, some of which were very unconventional. A total of 503 were built over nine years, adopting improvements of later production models. In addition, some USAF examples were equipped for the delivery of "special" weapons. Upgrades enabled the reconnaissance systems to remain capable, including the 1990 Gulf War. A limited air-to-air missile was added to some aircraft prior to retirement. The variant was also exported to Israel, South Korea and Spain. Several examples were also used in the drone program as QRF-4C. Equipped with smaller ground mapping radar.

F-4D

The F-4D supplemented the F-4C with the USAF. The F-4D systems were tuned more towards the strike role than the previous F-4C production. As with the F-4C, it served in Southeast Asia and later with the Air Force Reserve and the Air National Guard, retiring by the end of 1992. The only known variant was a quartet of EF-4D in the late sixties. Starting in early 1966, production totaled 825, with exports to Iran and South Korea.

F-4E

First flying in June 1967, the F-4E Phantom became the measuring stick for future fighters to compare to. The most noticeable feature was the gun under the nose. The lesson, that a gun was a necessity on fighter aircraft, had turned full circle. Over 1500 aircraft were built, including Japanese partially built total of 140 F-4EJ. The F-4E introduced (later) such items as wing slats, improved engines, radar, TISEO, etc to the USAF Phantom fleet. The F-4E led to the development of the German F-4F and the F-4EJ for Japan. The F-4E was exported to Australia, Egypt, Greece, Iran, Israel, South Korea and Turkey. In several batches, over 116 were converted to the F-4G Wild Weasel. Close to 200 examples of the F-4E and F-4G were converted to drones and expending as targets as QF-4E and QF-4G.

RF-4E

Reconnaissance aircraft built for export were designated RF-4E. General layout was based on the USAF RF-4C, with deliveries to Germany, Greece, Iran, Israel, Japan (as RF-4EJ) and Turkey. Equipped with J79-GE-17 engines with the longer burner cans.

F-4D of triple nickel at Udorn RTAFB, August 2, 1971. Photo courtesy of Larsen.

F-4D, 25 TFS, 8 TFW, Feb, 1971, Steel Tiger.

Rarely seen onboard a carrier, the F-4J Black Bunny, of VX-4, is seen here lining up dates for launch. Photo: Martin Collection.

66-669 482 TFW "FM" F-4D in Hill Gray II. Courtesy of Alex Rodriguez, Jr.

F-4D, 555TFS, 432TRW May 1970, Udorn RTAFB. Courtesy of Don Jay.

F-4EJ

Designation the for Japanese operated version of F-4E. A total of 96 upgraded to F-4EJ Kai standard and 17 to the RF-4EJ for the reconnaissance role.

F-4F

German Air Force production fighter and fighter-bomber, of which 175 were built. Various upgrade programs were completed including 110 to advanced ICE status. Originally lighter as some systems with several systems omitted.

F-4G

Designation of F-4G was used for the Wild Weasel conversions from the F-4E. All aircraft were taken from the FY69 production, replacing the F-105G Thunderchief. The F-4G was equipped and armed to clear a path through defenses of radar and SAM systems. Between 1975 and 1981, 116 F-4E were converted to F-4G standards. The gun was removed and replaced with a receiver faring. Various antennas were added over the airframe, including on top of the fin. This model was used extensively in the Gulf War. A reduced post Cold War fleet was passed to the National Guard before replacement by HARM toting advanced single seat F-16. Many were expired after conversion to as QF-4G.

F-4J

The F-4J was the final new production Phantom fighter for the USN and USMC. The F-4J had improved systems and capabilities. Most visually noticeable when compared to the F-4B, was the lack of a "chin" under the nose radar placement. This model featured fixed inboard slats, improved J79-GE-10 engines with the longer burner cans and other improvements. It served as the standard fleet fighter following the F-4B. The USN continued its "no gun" policy with the F-4J. A total of 522 were built starting in 1966. Close to 250 were upgraded to F-4S standard. Fifteen received enhancements and were supplied to the RAF as F-4J(UK) or Phantom F.3.

F-4K

US designation for 52 Phantom FG.1 ordered for the Royal Navy. Two were prototype YF-4K and 50 production aircraft. Aircraft were extensively modified with UK supplied engines and other equipment to Royal Navy requirements. The fitting of the Spey engines required a slightly wider fuselage plus a second set of Aux Air Doors above both engines.

F-4M

US designation for 118 Phantom FGR.2 ordered for the RAF. Two were prototype YF-4M and 116 production F-4M. As per the F-4K, the aircraft were heavily equipped with components to suit RAF (and UK industry) needs.

The Tiger Squadron, 141TFS/108TFW, NJ-ANG deployed to Bodo, Norway for 'Exercise Barefrost 89.' Here phantom 67-343 is seen banking over an Ice Glacier in Northern Norway. The 141 TFS/108 TFW, NJ-ANG. Courtesy of Don Spering/AIR.

F-4E, 34 TFS, 338TFW, January 1971. Operation Lam Song 719, Laos. Courtesy of Don Jay.

F-4G prototype at Edwards AFB in February 1976. Photo courtesy of D.R. Jenkins.

F-4E 22 TFS 36 TFW at the 1976 Tactical Air Meet at Twenthe, Netherlands, 10 May 1976. Photo Martin Collection.

Phancon 1993, "BH" RF-4C, Birmingham, AL, 1993. Courtesy of Alex Rodriquez, Jr.

This RF-4C 64-1056 piloted by Lt. Greg Muse checks drag chute area for obstructions/personnel before releasing drag chute, 28 August 1982. This Aircraft was lost during a Desert Storm mission in 1991. Courtesy of Mike Holloway.

On 1 May 81 RF-4C 65-0866 is elevated in paint bay for wraparound camo pattern application. Courtesy of Mike Holloway.

(Above and Below) 10 October 1970, 155800 VF-96. Mig-killing F-4J on 10 May 1972 by VF96 Cunningham/Driscoll. Courtesy of Akira Watanabe.

RF-4C from the 38 TRS 26 TRW at Ramstein AB, Germany on June 7, 1971. Photo courtesy of Dennis Hughes.

MiG-killing F-4J on 10 May 1972. Courtesy of Akira Watanabe.

F-4G, 69-0245. Courtesy of M.R. Hall.

F4G Buno 150492, VF-213 USS Kitty Hawk, winter 1965. Courtesy of V. Valentine.

F-4G, 39TFTS 35 TFW, November 1979, George AFB. Courtesy of Don Jay.

Hollomon F-4E landing at Kelly AFB in San Antonio, TX, 1996. Courtesy of Alex Rodriguez, Jr.

Tyndall AFB, FL. Standing next to QF-4E. Courtesy of D.R. Kuntz.

The end of an era, the Marine Unit at Andrews AFB shows of its star studded paint scheme. VMFA-321 flew the Phantom from 1973-1991. Col. Terry Duggan heads for the blue during a photo sortie. Courtesy of Don Spering/AIR.

F-4N

The F-4N was the result of a modernization program for the F-4B. A cable duct seen on the upper side of both intakes, coupled with the sensor under the radome, made for identification of the F-4N. The cable duct was not installed on the initial batch but were later retro fitted. The refit was extensive with ECM, engines and avionics all receiving upgrades, along with the VTAS helmet-mounted sight system. A total of 228 were done with airframes returning to service in early 1973. The type was replaced with the modified F-4S and early Hornets in remaining active and reserve formations. Many were later converted to the QF-4N drone configuration. These took on the role of the expendable QF-4B for missile trials and development work. The aircraft were capable of manned or unmanned flight. As the inventory of convertible F-4N Phantoms diminished the F-4S fleet was substituted.

SSGT Steve Wescott packs the chute, TSGT Ed Quinones puts BDU-33 practice bombs on the left TER as TSGT Steven Sabato and SSGT Ben Barnes work the cockpits. 108th Cams Personnel, life support, weapons and crew chiefs prepare 464 for one of the eight sorties she will fly to do her share of "108th Combat Surge-90" F-4E "NJ" 68-0464 141 TFS/108 TFW, NJ-ANJ MAFB-NJ record breaking sortie Surge, 127 sorties out of 128. 03-Nov-90. Courtesy of Steve Rogers/AIR.

F-4S

As the F-4B was converted into the F-4N, the F-4J fleet was modified and rebuilt into F-4S configuration. It was the last major type of the Phantom to serve with the USN and USMC. A total of 265 were modified with up-rated engines, internal systems, avionics, "zero-time" wing, wiring, smoke-less J79-GE-10B engines and AN/AWG-10A digital radar. All but the first couple dozen F-4S conversions had wing slats. The type continued in front line service and reserves until replaced by the Hornet and Tomcat by late 1992. The F-4S can be identified by the newly extended cable duct on the intakes and lack of chin sensor under the radome (as per the F-4J).

AUSTRALIA

No story of the Australian Phantom would be complete without mention of the F-111. The failure of the F-111 to be ready on time resulted in the short-term and perhaps reluctant start of the F-4E Phantoms use by the Royal Australian Air Force. The F-111 was not going to be ready when due in 1967 and the aging Canberra fleet required replacement. The fleet served for under three years starting in September 1970. Interestingly, 21 of the 23 survivors were later converted by the USAF to the F-4G Wild Weasel standard as they were all from FY69 stock.

Australian Phantoms were delivered and returned in the standard USAF tactical camouflage scheme. Australia was the shortest-term user of the Phantom.

EGYPT

To help compensate Egypt for withdrawn Arab aid, following its signature to the Camp David Accord in July 1979, it was agreed the Egyptian Air Force would receive 35 Phantoms. All were ex-USAF F-4E models and began to arrive in the same year. This was a real twist of fate, as the Egyptian Air Force had fought against Israeli Phantoms since 1969. This led to the situation where Egyptian pilots that had previously trained and fought with Eastern-bloc aircraft were now flying the Phantom.

Unfortunately, the Egyptian Phantom was not considered a success by most. In July 1980, to ease the type transition, the USAF deployed a squadron to Egypt for 90 days to assist in the training. Maintenance and aircraft serviceability plagued the Egyptian operated Phantom from the start. Several attempts were made to sell the fleet to Turkey, to fund the numbers of the less complicated and new Fighting Falcon. The idea of introducing a relatively small number of complex aircraft, in a hurry, to an air force operating far less complicated aerial systems proved too much at the time. Three further examples were provided to "top up" the fleet after 1989.

Phantoms supplied to the Egyptian Air Force were delivered in the standard USAF tactical camouflage scheme, later going through two of the gray schemes. In addition, the Egyptian Air Force applied large distinct yellow/orange areas to aid in aerial recognition.

McChord AFB in Washington State was used as a transit base for many Navy flights to the far east. This F-4B from VMFA-314 at rest in June 1975. Photo courtesy of Douglas Remington.

Australian F-4E Phantom, in standard tactical camouflage, awaits use at RAAF Amberely in May 1973. Photo Martin Collection.

GERMANY

German involvement with the Phantom began with a replacement of the RF-104G in the reconnaissance role within two wings. Eighty-eight RF-4E were contracted for, with the first delivered in January 1971. These aircraft served with both wings and test units and added the air-to-ground role after modifications started in 1978. With the collapse of the Soviet empire and the Warsaw Pact, coupled with the unification of East and West Germany, the RF-4E program was brought to a close. Both Greece and Turkey received ex-German reconnaissance Phantoms, deliveries of 27 to Greece starting in 1994 and 47 to Turkey starting the following year.

It had been thought the Starfighter replacement, the MRCA, would be in service by 1975. When it became apparent this was not going to happen, the German Air Force went looking to replace the Starfighter for both the fighter wings and two fighter-bomber wings. The initial plan was to procure a much lighter single seat variant, to be called the F-4F. In time, the conventional second crew member was retained with the aircraft lacking some major systems found on the standard F-4E. These included aerial refueling capability, leading edge slats, reduced fuel and the Sparrow missile system. The German Air Force was to receive 175 F-4F Phantoms.

The German Air Force used sites in the USA to work-up on the Phantom and later continual training. Initially eight F-4F Phantoms were maintained in the USA for training purposes. These were replaced in 1977 with ten new F-4E, freeing the F-4F for service in Europe. These aircraft moved to Holloman AFB in 1992, remaining until replaced by both F-4F and F-4F ICE seven years later.

In Germany, two fighter wings were equipped first taking priority over the fighter-bomber wings. The F-4F was upgraded under several projects adding a variety of weapons systems and refueling capability. With the next generation of fighters some time off, it became obvious the upgraded F-4F were no match for the latest, and then current, fighters. It was to become the most advanced production upgrade of any Phantom. The German Air Force proceeded with the ICE program. It included the latest radar from the Hornet, coupled with AIM-

This F-4F displays the standard greys finish used with darker topsides. Photo Martin Collection.

The upgraded German F-4F ICE aircraft can be identified by the lack of black radome. This aircraft was visiting Cambrai, France in mid 1996. Photo Martin Collection.

All German Phantoms were delivered in this splinter style camouflage of green and gray with silver undersides. This F-4F Phantom carried additional markings for the 1978 Tactical Weapons Meet at RAF Wildenrath. Photo Martin Collection.

Both Greece and Turkey maintained this scheme when the aircraft were transferred to the new owners, this former German RF-4E Phantom displays the lizard camouflage. Photo Martin Collection.

120 AMRAAM missiles in recess bays, along with many other systems. A total of 110 aircraft were to received the ICE features. With this upgrade, the Phantom will continue its service with the German Air Force well into the next century.

The original color scheme of all German Phantoms was the standard green and gray upper and silver lower surfaces. The RF-4E Phantoms later received a lizard tactical scheme consisting of three shades of green which they retained for the rest of their service life with the German Air Force.

In the early eighties there were a number of experimental schemes of varying shades of green and gray until the whole F-4F fleet was standardized on four shades of gray, primarily optimized for the air defense role. Two schemes were chosen and applied to the fleet, the first with straight edges when viewed from above and wavy from the side. The second appeared more wavy over all with less variations. One method of differentiating is the application of a straight edge on the tail for the former. Various F-4F were painted with bright colors on rudders, wing tips, fuselage spines for use in ACM and target duties.

When the F-4F ICE-program gained momentum another change occurred. The F-4F was now considered as purely air-air and thus received the current gray paint scheme. Of note is that ICE modified aircraft have a gray radome while the remainder of the fleet gray. The Holloman based Phantoms F-4F received the USAF Hill II scheme to facilitate maintenance and logistics along side with USAF Phantoms operating at Holloman AFB until late 1997.

GREECE

In 1971 the Greek government signed contracts for the delivery of 36 new Phantom F-4E aircraft. Deliveries began in March 1974 with an additional two attrition examples arriving in June 1976. Also in 1976, a second batch of 18 F-4E Phantoms were funded, along with an additional eight reconnaissance RF-4E.

Changing world conditions allowed the Greek Air Force to acquire a number of used Phantoms. In 1991, 28 ex-Air National Guard F-4E were provided to Greece as compensation for continued US use of bases in Greece. The Greek Air Force took advantage of acquiring further RF-4E reconnaissance platforms from the German Air Force. Starting in July 1994, up to 29 examples were acquired. An upgrade program was signed in 1997 with DASA of Germany providing many of the enhanced features of the F-4F ICE.

New F-4E and RF-4E were delivered to Greece in the standard USAF tactical camouflage scheme, while used aircraft came in various schemes including grays. The F-4E schemes were given up for the very smart looking gray-blue top color and lighter gray underside scheme unique for the Greek Air Force. The Phantoms going through the DASA upgrade were painted in a new three gray wrap around scheme. The ex-German Air Force aircraft were maintained, at least for several years, in the black and two green camouflage scheme.

IRAN

Phantoms purchased by the regime of the Shah for the IIAF have seen operational service only paralleled by US and Israel forces. The IIAF was the second largest foreign user of the Phantom. The initial batch of 32 F-4D were delivered starting in September 1968. The reconnaissance RF-4E started arriving in February 1971 with the gun toting F-4E, the next month. A total of 177 F-4E and 16 RF-4E Phantoms were delivered to Iran.

The total would have been larger except for stoppage due to the fall of the Shah and rise of the Islamic Fundamentalist Revolution. A further 31 F-4E and 16 RF-4E were canceled in February 1979. The IIAF had used the Phantom to assist the Oman Forces in 1975, including one loss. Without continued US assistance, the fleets operational rates declined. The IRIAF fleet was put to the test over the eight year war against Iraq. The original ten squadrons have been much reduced by losses and cannibalization of airframes to maintain the remaining aircraft. Various home grown solutions have been used to increase, or at least maintain flyable numbers of the Phantom. For example, the use of a Chinese anti-ship missile on the Phantom could have been in a fiction novel years ago, but became reality. The foreign parts supply has also been a tale of secrets involving, according to mixed sources, the United States, Israel and European nations

Iranian Phantoms were standard green and two tan scheme, maintaining a light gray underside. Although current IRIAF photos of the Phantom are not common there does appear to be a change.

ISRAEL

It could be said the Israeli use of the Phantom began in a storm and has, in over thirty years use, continued to play a major role in the Middle East. Following the 1967 Six Day War, the United States stepped in as a weapons supplier to Israel. Starting in late 1969, the first of 44 new F-4E and six RF-4E Phantoms arrived in Israel. There have been stories of ex-USN F-4B delivered to Israel back in 1962, without confirmation. Within weeks of delivery the Phantoms were used in the War of Attrition, along the Suez Canal and into Egypt. Further batches of six, 18 and twelve F-4E were added during 1970 and 1971. Two examples of the RF-4C were also added in 1970. In the 19 months prior to the next round of warfare in the Middle East, a further 24 used F-4E were sent to Israel. New aircraft in the form of 18 F-4E and six RF-4E, were also provided in the same period. Deliveries were the latest upgraded production examples possible.

During the 1973 Israel-Arab war, over 37 Phantoms were lost in combat. During the conflict additional Phantoms were ferried into the country and went directly into service. At least 34 examples of the F-4E are known to have taken this route, with the real number higher. The Phantom was used on several fronts and extended combat use in some not so conventional warfare. At least another 24 used and 24 new F-4E arrived in Israel in the next three years. The reconnaissance role was bolstered by twelve new RF-4E as well. The real totals may never be known, as Israeli censorship remains. It has been generally excepted that over 200 F-4E have seen service and at least 26 RF-4C/E reconnaissance platforms. It was also excepted that close to 60 have been lost, including at least 33 in the 1973 conflict. Even since then, the Phantom has seen plenty of use in the Middle East with a series of clashes over Lebanon, occupied territories and the northern security zone.

As the type aged and newer fighters entered service, the Phantom was used as a heavy fighter-bomber, passing the air-defense and straight fighter role to the F-15 and F-16. The type was to be passed to reserve formations with the arrival of the indigenous Lavi. When this plan fell through, further new US built fighters were acquired and the Phantom fleet was to be upgraded.

The adoption of many home-grown systems has allowed Israeli industry to offer upgrades to other Phantom users, including the Turkish Air Force. The fleet had over the years received various upgrades and enhancements, including air-to-air and air-to-ground weapons. The most advanced of these was the Super Phantom or Kurnass 2000 conversion from the F-4E. Highlights include the latest technology computers, avionics suit and structural work. One prototype was even flown with a completely new set of engines. Unless the Middle East finds peace, the Phantom will continue going into harms way in this region.

Israeli F-4E Phantom fleet was delivered in the colors associated with nearly all combat types of the IAF, green and two tans, with a light gray-blue underside. The changes to this appearance varied little over the years. During the 1973 emergency resupply effort, F-4E were delivered and fought in the standard USAF tactical scheme with only the markings over painted. Many of the RF-4C received gray paint schemes.

JAPAN

The Japanese government purchased 140 F-4EJ Phantoms to up grade its air defense capability and in part to replace the F-104 Starfighter. Two examples were built and flown to Japan, the remainder built under license with some components supplied by McDonnell. The main mission of the Japanese Air Self-Defense Force is in the title, as such systems are selected for that purpose. Notable changes to the F-4EJ were the omission of aerial refueling gear, sparrow missile systems and other equipment not

Japanese Phantoms carried wild colored identification markings for ACM and target-towing operations. This displays the target system and orange markings on top of the standard early scheme in November 1982. Photo Kikuo Nakane via Martin Collection.

This F-4E Phantom was photographed at Elgin AFB in September 1971 on its delivery flight to Iran, with temporary USAF markings. Photo Martin Collection.

Japanese reconnaissance Phantoms were designated RF-4EJ and initially painted in this brown, green and tan upper surfaces, with light gray undersides scheme. This colorful machine was displayed at the July 1987 Hyakuri. Photo Masanori Ogawa via Martin Collection.

This F-4E Phantom of the South Korean Air Force was attending Red Flag exercises in September 1990 at Nellis AFB. Photo Marty Isham via Martin Collection.

In typical Spanish sunshine, this F-4C Phantom displays the standard scheme used for the fleet, during May 1992. Photo Daniel Loreille via Martin Collection.

consistent with objectives at the time. Six squadrons were to be formed and operate the interceptor F-4EJ from Japan.

Over the years the fleet has seen various upgrades including avionics, weapons and radar, reversing earlier decisions. Several of the omitted systems were applied to the Phantom as the need arose and it became acceptable to do so. In the latest upgrade 96 airframes were maintained. The Phantom was even given a limited anti-ship role as part of the upgrading process. The next generation of fighter, through the F-15 Eagle, finished replacing the F-104 Starfighter and supplemented, but did not entirely replace the Phantom in the air defense role.

In addition to the original purchase, 14 purchased RF-4E airframes were built in the USA. These aircraft also underwent various upgrades. With the arrival of the F-15 Eagle, and an on going desire to increase reconnaissance assets, 17 former interceptors were converted into RF-4EJ, maintaining the gun but adding a center line pod.

The initial paint scheme for the F-4EJ Phantom was gray, with white undersides. By 1980 an overall darker gray was in use. Numerous wild color applications in the form of stripes, blocked areas, and even full aircraft designs have been painted on JASDF Phantoms as a matter of regular course. No other air force has used such a wild variety of colors and shapes on Phantoms.

The intent of the schemes was to provide visual assistance during ACM exercises. The reconnaissance RF-4E started with upper surfaces finished in brown, green and tan, with light gray undersides. This was later changed to upper colors similar to the USAF Euro 1 scheme, with two greens and dark gray on the upper surfaces.

KOREA

Korean skies have been no stranger to the Phantom. The ongoing "undeclared peace" following the Korean War saw numerous deployments of USAF Phantoms as part of the support for the South Korean Government. A group of 18 ex-USAF F-4D arrived in Korea in August 1969 as a trade to the RoKAF for 36 F-5A/B which were transferred to South Vietnam. Deliveries continued with up to 92 seeing RoKAF service. The F-4E arrived in 1988 with up to 30 used aircraft noted, plus 37 new built aircraft. Further deliveries have boosted the total to over 100 F-4E. The reconnaissance Phantom was added to the inventory with up to 27 used RF-4C aircraft delivered. Various upgrades have been under study.

The Korean Phantom fleet was delivered in USAF tactical camouflage, changing to various home-grown gray schemes in the nineties.

SPAIN

The first Spanish contact with the Phantom was through a USAF based wing at Torrejon AB. This USAF wing used the F-4E, then the F-4C in late 1973 and finally the F-4D in 1978 and 1979. During the 1971 shuffling of USAF Phantom assets in Europe the Spanish Air Force, the Ejercito del Aire received the first of a total of 36 F-4C Phantoms. In 1978, a further four examples were provided along with four RF-4C. The F-4C was replaced by the F-18A/B by April 1979, some continuing until late 1990 in non-operational roles. A further eight used reconnaissance RF-4E which arrived in 1989.

The F-4C fleet was received, operated and retired in the standard USAF two greens and tan upper surface, with light gray underside scheme. The RF-4C fleet adopted an overall gray scheme, but also use the "Hill II" scheme.

TURKEY

Forty F-4E Phantoms were ordered in 1973 for use with the Turkish Air Force. Four years later a second batch, this time 32 aircraft were ordered. In 1981, 1984, 1986 and 1987, batches of 15, 15, 15 and 40 used F-4E Phantoms were obtained from the USAF. A second batch of 40 used aircraft was provided in 1991 as a result of co-operation during the Gulf War. Further deliveries of used F-4E continued in the nineties reaching over 230 in total. Eight new RF-4E were also provided after 1977. These were followed by 47 used aircraft from Germany. It should be noted many of the aircraft were acquired for use as spares. A broad based upgrade program has been launched to enhance a portion of the F-4E fleet through Israeli firms. This includes radar and new weapons generally in parallel with the Kurnass 2000 IDF/AF.

The Turkish Air Force maintained its Phantom fleet in the schemes they were received in, including the ex German RF-4E reconnaissance machines.

UNITED KINGDOM - ROYAL NAVY

The Royal Navy was to procure the Phantom for its fleet carriers with an order for 52 FG.1 aircraft to replace the twin-boom Sea Vixen. When the P.1154 was canceled the void was to be filled by the Phantom FG.1. The British Phantoms were to be powered by the Spey engine, which even after its expensive fit to the Phantom was never considered ideal. Although it had advantages in some regards, the small number built proved very expensive. The first aircraft flew in 1966.

The deck length of Royal Navy carriers was considerably shorter than the design parameters for the USN Phantoms, thus the Royal Navy aircraft had, among other refinements, the nose gear lengthened to perform steeper and slower approaches. The intent was to operate the Phantoms from at least two of Britain's three carriers. A fire on one accelerated the retirement leaving only one to operate the Phantom. Half the fleet went directly to RAF service on delivery, the remainder following the retirement of the carrier in late 1978.

Royal Navy Phantoms were retained in dark sea gray with white undersides during service. Some were noted in the early RAF scheme during transfers between the two services.

UNITED KINGDOM - ROYAL AIR FORCE

The British use of the Phantom was the result of a complicated set of circumstances, at least for the RAF, that prior to it happening could easily be the result of fiction writing. The RAF "plan" was to introduce the Hawker P.1154 for inter-theater strike. This was on track until a change in government proved disastrous for the RAF and industry alike. When this program fell the became more acceptable as it had already been chosen by the Royal Navy.

The Phantom FGR.2 severed in the strike role with the RAF in Germany before replaced by the Jaguar in the mid-seventies. This released the Phantom fleet for service in the air defense role in both the UK and in Germany, generally replacing the very short range Lightning. Weapon systems were developed for the new role, while the reconnaissance role and mud moving weapons were passed to the Jaguar and Harrier.

Fifteen retired USN F-4J Phantoms were overhauled in the USA to boost the RAF Phantom fleet. Attrition and the need to deploy numbers of the Phantom FGR.2 to the recaptured Falkland Islands created a shortage of air defense assets for the RAF. These aircraft were far from fully converted to British standards and were thought of, from the start as short term service assets and only used by one squadron. The Phantom was replaced by the Tornado F.3 in the air defense role starting in 1988 with the last squadron giving up the Phantom in 1992.

The initial Phantom deliveries were in the RAF standard tactical camouflage of dark sea gray and dark green with light gray undersides. When the task switched to air defense only, the fleet was painted in light greasy, including the F.3 aircraft.

UNITED STATES NAVY

From the first deployment onboard a carrier in 1960, it was clear the Navy had a fighter with greatly enhanced capabilities, a major leap ahead of the previous fighter generation. From 1961 through 1986 the Phantom, through four basic versions, provided the aerial umbrella for the US fleet around the globe. Over two dozen units converted to the Phantom for fleet duty. These units were deployed in pairs onboard carriers, with air defense as the primary duty. There are numerous photos of Phantoms "escorting" Soviet long range aircraft. The Phantom saw extensive duty over Vietnam mainly operating

The RAF Phantom fleet was painted in gray for the air defense role. This FGR.2 was visiting RAF Wattisham in January 1992. The all blue tail was a special squadron marking. Photo Martin Collection.

The 1972 rather wet open house was the setting for this Phantom FG.1 showing the unique extended nose gear. Photo Martin Collection.

The "Hill II" scheme is applied to this Spanish Air Force RF-4C Phantom during a visit to the Netherlands in 1996. Photo Martin Collection.

Courtesy of C.W. Basso.

F-4J before being painted to represent the "Blue Angel" Scheme A/C#153812. Naval Air Test Center. Courtesy of Wayne Smith.

F-4J after being painted in "Blue Angel" Sheme. Courtesy of Wayne Smith.

from carriers in the fighter and fighter-bomber roles. Operations from within the Gulf of Tonkin and the entire length of Vietnam, kept carrier assets of the United States Navy more than heavily deployed and in harms way. Several other shore based units on both coasts handled training functions.

The "Blue Angels" demonstration team used the F-4J Phantom between January 1969 and August 1973 in an over all blue scheme with yellow trim.

The arrival of the Tomcat, in the early seventies, with its great "reach out and touch" radar and Phoenix missile system, began the draw down of the fleet Phantom units. Two squadrons were converted to the Hornet. At least five reserve units flew the Phantom staring in 1967, the last retired in May 1987.

The last location to fly, or operate the USN Phantom was NAS Point Mugu. Operations, manned and unmanned, continue to expend the remaining QF-4N and QF-4S in the drone program. Like the USAF Phantom, the Navy Phantom will continue in the "Targets-R-Us" role for years.

The initial paint scheme for USN and USMC Phantoms was gray with white undersides and moveable surfaces, as was standard on most US naval types for decades. This evolved into an overall gray and then on to TPS of mixed grays overall. Colorful markings were very much reduced and almost non-existent by the TPS scheme. There were other schemes used by the reserve units including a splinter "Ferris like" scheme.

UNITED STATES MARINE CORPS

Over 15 active and four reserve USMC squadrons operated the fighter versions of the Phantom. The F-4B and F-4J were followed by the converted F-4N and F-4S models into service. Two further squadrons provided training capabilities. Although occasionally deployed on carriers, the USMC fleet generally operated from land bases. During the conflict in Southeast Asia Marine Corps rotated numerous squadron in-country providing support to ground forces. The Phantom continued to provide the back bone of Marine Corps aviation in the fighter and tactical roles until the eighties and the arrival of the F-18 Hornet.

The RF-4B operated in the reconnaissance role both onboard carriers and land bases. The Phantom complemented the Crusader in this role, as the USN did not operate the RF-4B. At first the fleet was divided between three units. They were consolidated into one in 1975 and remained as such until retirement in 1990.

The USMC generally followed the same schemes as those of the USN. The Marine Corps never seemed short of colorful paint, as most squadrons embellished their mounts with a very colorful marking.

UNITED STATES AIR FORCE

While the number of aircraft developed for USN to reach service in the USAF are few, the Phantom proved in numbers and service to be an excellent investment. The F-110A, as the initial Air Force Phantom was known, began with two wings at MacDill AFB in Florida. The F-4C (after the 1962 tri-service redesignation) was followed by the F-4D in the aerial and fighter-bomber role. In time, through several versions, the Phantom served in every theater of operations.

In and around Vietnam, the Phantom was used extensively resulting in the lose of hundreds. The aircraft proved superior to many other types deployed in similar roles. The experience saw vast numbers of the F-4C, F-4D and F-4E in use. The RF-4C along with the RF-101 Voodoo provided the bulk of Air Force tactical aerial reconnaissance platforms during the conflict. It also led to the development and deployment of the gun equipped F-4E and much later the F-4G. The F-4G Wild Weasel program was designed to replaced the F-105G in the defense suppression role, with lessons learned during the conflict.

In Europe, several NATO assigned wings converted to the Phantom in the sixties proving to be the envy of other NATO forces. The ability to carry greater loads, over greater distances, provided an edge. As each improved version was introduced to the USAF, NATO assigned units were a priority. With the real threat from the Warsaw Pact the Phantom helped provide a balance. Until the advent of the F-15 Eagle and F-16 Falcon, the Phantom was the premier fighter aircraft for the USAF in Europe. Even after these new generation fighters replaced the Phantom in most roles, the RF-4C and F-4G continued for several years.

Numerous Air Force Reserve and Air National Guard units equipped with the Phantoms. The F-4C, F-4D and F-4E providing assets for air defense in addition to "mud-moving", reconnaissance and finally with the Wild Weasel. The Phantom remained in service long enough to see RF-4C and the F-4G in the 1990 "non-competitive" Gulf War.

In CONUS numerous wings were equipped with the Phantoms. As the age of the "teen-series" fighter came, the Phantom was passed to the Air Force Reserve and Air National Guard. In general the F-15 Eagle replaced the Phantom in air defense and the F-16 in other roles. This trend continued through reserve units after regular service units had converted. The "Thunderbirds" aerial demonstration team used the F-4E between June 1969 and 1973. Selected aircraft had the gun and radar units removed and replaced with 400 pounds of lead, as ballast.

The last remaining flying USAF Phantom fleet has been employed in the aerial target program, flying from Holloman AFB and Tyndall AFB. This involves conversions, for unmanned flights of RF-4C, F-4E and F-4G adding the Q prefix on completion.

As first introduced into service, the F-110A (F-4C) and RF-4C Phantoms were painted in gull gray with white undersides. By the late sixties the age of tactical camouflage had arrived with upper surfaces painted in two greens and tan, with the under surfaces in light gray. This evolved into wrap-around, eliminating the gray by extending the upper colors to the underside. The next step was the "Euro 1" camouflage with two greens and charcoal gray in a wrap-around scheme. Aircraft serving in the air defense role used an overall gray scheme.

With the adoption of the F-16 in the mid eighties, a new scheme was introduced based on the three grays of the F-16 called "Hill I". This scheme was dark gray overall from the rear canopy back, with a lighter gray for the tail, outer wings, upper nose and horizontal stabilizer. The underside was painted in an even lighter gray. There were various deviation to this. The "Hill II" scheme removed the underside lightest gray, extended the dark gray down the canopy sides incorporating the anti-glare panel. It was also applied to most of the underside.

F-4D, Jay Hawks 66-553, 184TFG, KS-ANG Phantom close-out, 31 March 1990. The last F-4 to leave, 184TFG personnel take their turn at signing this 553 McConnell AFB, KS. Courtesy of Don Spering/AIR.

Special Stories of the F-4 Phantom II

F-4C early Weasel of the 67 TFS 18 TFW at Korat RTAFB, November 13, 1972. Photo courtesy of Larsen.

PHANTOM RIDE AT NAS POINT MUGU
by Bill Kelly

I have never been a military flyer, but during 1982, with two years of college to go, I held a summer job as an engineering intern at the Pacific Missile Test Center (PMTC), Point Mugu NAS, CA. It was through this temporary position and the generous enthusiasm of a Navy lieutenant commander, whom I befriended, that I was lucky enough to receive a back seat ride in a Navy F-4J, Bureau Number 153073.

As the school year came to a close and warm summer weather beckoned, I happily packed my bags, eager to begin my three month adventure at Point Mugu. Upon arriving at PMTC I was assigned to the Fighter Weapons Branch of the Flight Test Division located in a large hangar and office complex next to the main runway. While the F-14 and its weapons were the focal point of the flight test work at that time, PMTC also employed several veteran F-4's as support aircraft. All the PMTC aircraft sported a bright blue band across their tails, superimposed with a distinctive triangular shield, that distinguished them from the other aircraft on he field. The sights and sounds were truly exciting as I settled into my daily ground job of monitoring telemetry data for Sparrow missile tests, in addition to being a general gopher for the technical staff and Navy flyers. It was during the course of this routine that I met Lt. Cmdr. Bob Kelly.

Bob Kelly was a seasoned Navy Radar Intercept Officer (RIO) who had come up through the Phantom and was also current in the Tomcat. After I was on the job for a few weeks, the friendly and outgoing lieutenant commander realized that I was a hopeless airplane nut, especially enamored with the F-4 and all of its exploits. Of course, I never dreamed I would actually have the opportunity fly in the back seat of an F-4, so when Bob told me he might be able to arrange a ride for me, I was nearly in a state of shock. Nevertheless, Bob pulled the right strings. I went to the altitude chamber and rode the ejection seat trainer, which was a thrill in itself. I was qualified for the flight, but it would be another two weeks before the big day arrived.

Although it was now September and I had already returned to my college courses in Los Angeles, I gladly made the two hour drive back to Point Mugu for my ride in the Phantom. That afternoon offered a spectacular sky with brilliant sunshine and excellent visibility. It was the top one percent of autumn weather on the California coast where low clouds often lingered on less perfect days. When I arrived, I met my pilot, Lt. Cmdr. Pelham Mills, a no nonsense gentleman who gave me the impression with great enthusiasm, that we were going to have some real airborne fun. After gathering up my borrowed flight gear, we headed off to the flight line. As a bonus, we were to be paired up with a PTC F-14 during part of our flight. After 18 years I must admit that I do not recall how this last detail came to be, but it certainly added to the excitement and I was glad I had remembered to bring my camera.

My F-4J #153073 was the third aircraft produced in the first block of the "J" models and was delivered to the Navy in 1966. It had functioned primarily as a flying test bed, alternating between places like Patuxent River, St. Louis, Baltimore and Point Mugu over the years. This F-4 was also somewhat unique in that, because it lacked many of the external ECM antennas and other protuberances added to most Navy Phantoms, it was an especially clean looking jet. Also, its engines appeared to be of the earlier type normally fitted to F-4B's, with the shorter exhaust nozzles. As we approached the big bird, a ground crewman helped me strap into the back seat. I was instructed where to find the sick sack, but I hoped I would not need it. Soon Pelham had the Phantom's engines rumbling like those of a locomotive and I became acutely aware that I was strapped to the front of a tremendous amount of mass.

As we taxied out of the chocks and headed for the northeast runway, the F-14 came alongside from his ramp on the other end of the air station. While the two jets paused short of the runway, Pelham pushed the throttles up on the mighty J-79s one at a time to run the necessary pre-takeoff checks. We then taxied onto the runway with the F-14 slightly behind and to our right. For a few seconds we sat, poised, waiting for takeoff clearance. All the flight gear I was wearing felt a bit cumbersome and the Martin Baker seat felt more like a rock, but at that point I was happier to be in that seat than anywhere else in the world.

Finally, the F-4's engines began to spool up, the brakes were released and we were on our way. A few seconds later the afterburners provided an additional thump on the backside. The acceleration was impressive, but unlike a powerful automobile where acceleration is brief, in the Phantom is seemed unrelenting, more like riding a rocket if one can imagine that. In short order the nose gear was off the pavement, then the mains and we were airborne, gear up, accelerating 50 feet over the runway with the air station boundary approaching fast. We had attained a considerable amount of speed when Pelham pulled up tightly to the left in a chandelle type maneuver. I could feel the g-suit beginning to squeeze my lower body and I was pushed down in the seat, but I managed to look over my left shoulder and clearly spot the F-14 at seven o'clock, about one quarter mile in trail. Our steep left hand turn continued until we rolled out on a heading to take us over the ocean and the picturesque Channel Islands. About the time we crossed the coastline, Pelham pulled the hungry engines out of afterburner and he asked me if I was doing okay. As I replied in the affirmative, he told me that he would do an easy roll. For the next two or three seconds the sky smoothly twisted around the nose. It felt so effortless, so graceful! I was wearing a huge grin!

During the next 15 minutes or so, we flew in formation with the F-14. I was afforded some excellent photo opportunities as the Tomcat flew box patterns around us under a perfect blue sky. When the time came for the F-14 to leave, he lit both burners and pulled up and over the top in an immelmann. What sight, but we were not done yet. Now on our own, Pelham was about to show me some of what the F-4 was capable of. His first maneuver was a loop, followed by huge barrel roll, each initiated at a speed of about 600 knots and consuming perhaps 7,000 to 8,000 feet vertically. The old Phantom could definitely eat up a lot of sky and while I had experience significant g-forces before in light plane aerobatics, the difference with the F-4 was the duration. Of course, every performance needed a grand finale, which for us was an afterburner corkscrew climb, which, as I recall, took us to more than 30,000 feet. I was impressed by the old bird and by Pelham Mills, but jet fuel does not last forever, so we started back toward the roost.

Because a C-130 was in the traffic pattern at Point Mugu, we were unable to do an energetic fighter type "break" to the downwind, but this flight had exceeded my expectations by any measure. The touchdown on the runway was typically Navy, on the mark. As we cleared to the taxiway, the canopies came up and that cool coastal breeze came drifting in. It felt good. When we had pulled into the chocks and shut down, I asked the ground crew to take a picture of Pelham and myself in the cockpits. Although they were happy to oblige, when the shutter button on my camera was pushed, nothing happened. I had unwittingly already taken my last picture! So, I never got the "crew shot" and it is a blunder for which I have never forgiven myself. Oh well. I still cannot complain and I never needed that sick sack.

On year later in 1983, I served as a summer intern at Point Mugu for the last time, but I never got another ride in the F-4. Although I wanted to become a Naval Aviator, I always needed some correction to my vision, so flying in the front seat was not an option. Today I am a pilot at a regional airline on the west coast, but my wild ride in the brutish Phantom will forever be in a class by itself. Thanks Bob Kelly, for making one dream come true.

PHANTOM PHABLE
by Wayne Johnson

It was April 1972 and I had joined the "Black Knights" of VMFA-314 at MCAS El Toro only a few months earlier as a fire-control radar tech. One day a bunch of us were sitting on the deck, leaning against the hanger doors, waiting for one of our hops to return. We saw two smokers inbound and figured they were our birds. After they landed we could hear the J79s but couldn't see the birds taxiing as we were still sitting down. Then, looking over the Phantoms on our ramp, we saw the top of the vertical stabilizers, looking like shark fins in the water as our birds came down the taxiway. They started to do a 180 off the taxiway onto our ramp. We all stood up and our jaws hit the deck. By now, none of us wanted to take this debrief. As we headed off for Maintenance Control we were relieved to see that the Radar Shop NCOIC was already there and he would be the one to chat with the crew about why their bird left for the hop with the radome attached and returned with the radome GONE!

Epilogue: This bird was engaged in 1 v 1 ACM off the California coast. While pulling a

Courtesy of W. Johnson.

max G turn, there was a sudden onset of vibration and buffeting. The pilot rolled out level and the other bird joined up and informed Victor Whiskey 03 that his radome was gone. All the gages were okay and a visual by the wingman looked otherwise okay, so they headed back to El Toro. Near as anyone could tell, the causal factor was an overtorque of the cone bolts that secure the radome. There was one sergeant in the Radar Shop that had a habit of doing pull-ups on the 1/4 inch breaker-bar that was used to torque the radome. The moral of the story is that you can have too much of a good thing and that when the book says 120 in. lbs.; that's what they really mean. The good news was that the crew was okay, the bird got back and the damage wasn't too bad.

I had two tours with 314, totaling about 5-1/2 years. We lost four birds and two crews during that time. Capts. Lahlum, Maher, Duncan and Lt. Towle, we have not forgotten.

PHANTOM MEMORIES
by Alex Hrapunov

The day in 1969 when I saw firsthand the Thunderbird's Diamond formation "pass in review" down the flightline is the day I became a Phan. Since that day I've had many memorable experiences with the Rhino:

Listening to the scream of an F-4 on final approach to landing as the pilot controls the sound so as not to disturb those who don't appreciate it's beauty.

Witnessing the crash of the Thunderbird at the 1972 Air Transpo held at Dulles International Airport; seeing the F-4E stand on its tail before plummeting to the ground and the huge fireball rising up from behind the tree line. Hoping, but not knowing, whether the pilot got out; hearing a fellow attendee say they saw the glistening of the canopy as the pilot ejected and thinking "great, he got out!" On the way home nearing Andrews AFB, just as the announcement was made on the radio that the Thunderbird pilot was killed, seeing the Blue Angel Delta formation on final approach to touchdown.

Chuckling every time the roar of either the DC ANG or VMFA-321 F-4s in full burner on takeoff, setting off just about every car alarm in the vicinity on base.

And a whole lot of other memories, both good and bad.

It's been over 30 years since that day in 1969 when I witnessed the power and majesty of the Phantom firsthand and as I recall what I witnessed that day, I just smile.

A DIFFERENT KIND OF WAR STORY
by Val Valentine

We didn't always fly to/from the boat for any number of reasons. Alternates included garden spots such as Da Nang and Tan Son Nhut, RVN.

One of my favorite stories took place at the Doom (Da Nang Open Officer's Mess) Club. There was a stunning, beautiful, blonde-haired, blue-eyed lady reporter by the name of Elaine Shepherd visiting at Da Nang at the time of this incident. Of course, everyone was trying to get next to her because the only round-eyed women we had seen in a long time were either under the age of 11 or married to someone that outranked us!

We soon found out that she was sweet lady and quite adept at handling our raging hormones.

Anyway, on this particular day, she was interviewing us in the "O" Club, asking our names, where we were from and what type of aircraft/missions we were flying as well as any messages that she could take back to our families stateside.

Everything was going quite smoothly until this one Air Force Puke walked in and sat down for a brewski. By the time he showed up, Elaine had already spoken with most of us and was bellied up to the bar with us while we consumed mass quantities.

Elaine noticed this solitary Airman sitting by himself and realizing she had not yet spoken with him, went over and sat down. Once again, Elaine went through her usual questions only to find that the pilot in question refused to identify the type of aircraft and/or missions flown. By now, those of us at the bar were more than just a little interested as we knew what type of aircraft this AF Puke flew!

Well, one thing led to another and we figured out that this Whiskey Delta was trying to get the track on Elaine. One of his lines was that if he told her, he'd have to kill her.

As we listened more closely to their conversation, the AF pilot finally agreed to tell Elaine about his aircraft and the missions he was flying. His opening gambit was as follows, "Have you ever heard about the U-2?" to which Elaine replied, "Yes, that's a secret spyplane, isn't it?" His reply, "Yes, well I fly the U-3, it's 50 percent more secret that the U-2!"

When we heard this, several of us grabbed him, dragged him outside and threw him in the pool. Elaine came running out yelling at us until we explained to her that the U-3 was the military version of the Cessna 210 and this guy was just flying inter-theater "ash 'n trash" missions. She was so P. O.'d that she started yelling at the guy, grabbed a bunch of empty beer bottles and started throwing them at him when he was still in the pool.

We laughed so hard that we could hardly stand up, it was quite a sight!

TRANSITION TO THE F-4
by Val Valentine

In 1965 I transitioned into F-4s. It was quite a change from flying F-8s in all manners except acceleration. In those days, the F-4 had been in the fleet about five years; however, ACM (air combat maneuvering) tactics hadn't been fully developed for the aircraft and top gun was still two years away.

In the F-8 community, we had a saying, "When you're out of F-8s, you're out of fighters!" Har de har har.

In the F-4 community, we would soon find ourselves jousting with North Vietnam MiGs that weighted less than our internal fuel. It was very enlightening, if not downright dangerous to find a MiG on your six o'clock knowing that you couldn't turn with him and that the only way to shake him was to unload the aircraft, i.e. put the nose down and stroke full afterburner or go into a high speed or low speed yo yo to force him to overshoot or disengage. The good thing about having those two humongous J-79 engines (34,2000 pounds of thrust) was that there wasn't an aircraft flying in those days (except an F-105) that could catch or even get close to an F-4 going downhill in full burner.

Although you generally flew with the same RIO (radar intercept officer), I always briefed my back seater that I would never, repeat, never say any word that begins with "e" except for eject. With the understanding that if he heard the word eject that he would sequence himself and depart the aircraft before he heard the whole word.

Like the DC-10, the F-4 had its hydraulic lines for all three systems (PC1, PC2 and utility) routed side by side. Chances were if your aircraft took some heavy battle damage that affected your hydraulics, you lost all three systems, just like Sioux City. The anomaly of total hydraulic failure in the F-4 was that the stick would lock full aft, the aircraft would try to stand on its tail and would not respond to any control inputs. Further problems included the aircraft being fitted with Martin Baker MK4b (100/100) seats that required 100 KTS forward airspeed and 100 feet altitude and a maximum of 60 degree angle of bank, otherwise the seat wouldn't fire.

This particular story takes place in the Spring 1967 over North Vietnam. North Vietnam was divided into seven route packages, numbered 1 through 6A. The numbering started at the DMZ as Route Pack 1, the higher the number, the nastier the target. Hanoi was in RP6 and Haiphong was in RP 6A.

Vinh was North Vietnam's second largest seaport after Haiphong. Vinh was located in RP3 and consisted of many high value targets including manufacturing and major railyards.

We were flying a joint USAF/USN strike package against the railyards at Vinh. The flak was pretty nasty, they were throwing 23, 57 and 88mm flak up, generally you learned to tell the size by the shape and color of the puff and sometimes you could hear or feel small particles of metal bounding off your aircraft as you flew through it.

I was flight lead of an element of four Navy F-4s and we were loaded with the usual air to air garbage, i.e. 2-Aim 9B heat seeking sidewinders and 2-Aim 7B riding Sparrows which weren't good for much besides smoothing out the airflow on the underside of the aircraft. Each aircraft was fitted with a TER (triple ejecting rack) on each wing, which in turn were loaded with 3-MK 82 Snakeyes (500 pound high drag/low altitude release bomb).

Ahead of us, the Air Force had done a pretty good job of lighting up the targets and it

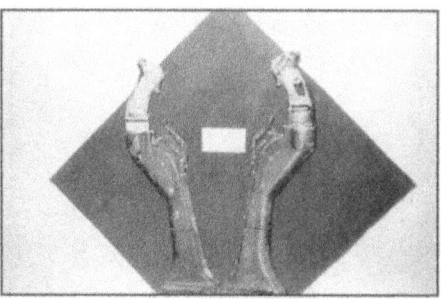

The Vietnamese AF Museum in Hanoi 1995-96 had F-4 joy sticks on display. Courtesy George Petersen.

LTCol Wayne Yarolem (Fighter Pilot) holds the record for the most hours flown by a Phantom pilot. 6514.6 total. Wayne's first flight 8 June 1967 in an F-4C 66-0232 and his last flight 8 June 1991 was in an Egyptian Phantom 67-0220. Almost twenty-five years in the Phantom cockpit. Wayne file assignments in the F-4 in 11 countries and over forty Sqn/wings. 392 combat sorties and 776 combat hours and 392 combat sorties. Courtesy of Don Spering/AIR.

didn't take rocket science to figure out that Sam and Charlie were going be mad at us for messing up their railyards and associated rolling stock.

We were still feet wet (over water) when I split my flight into 2-2 ship element, I then directed the second element to roll in on the railyards ahead of us and we would follow them in. My wingman was Ken Van Leuven from Ketchum, ID and his backseater, Donny Tucker from Dallas. I always liked Ken flying my wing as he was utterly predictable. The kind of aviator that if you screwed up and plowed into a mountain, there would be two holes—not just one.

In any event, we were at about 10,000 feet flying "loose deuce" as we weren't feet dry when I called for a 4-G vertical conversion. We rolled our aircraft inverted, pulled the noses through at a slant angle of 40 degrees and rolled out doing about 400 knots in full afterburner, it must have been a hell of a sight for the Vietnamese gunners.

Our ordnance load dictated that we would

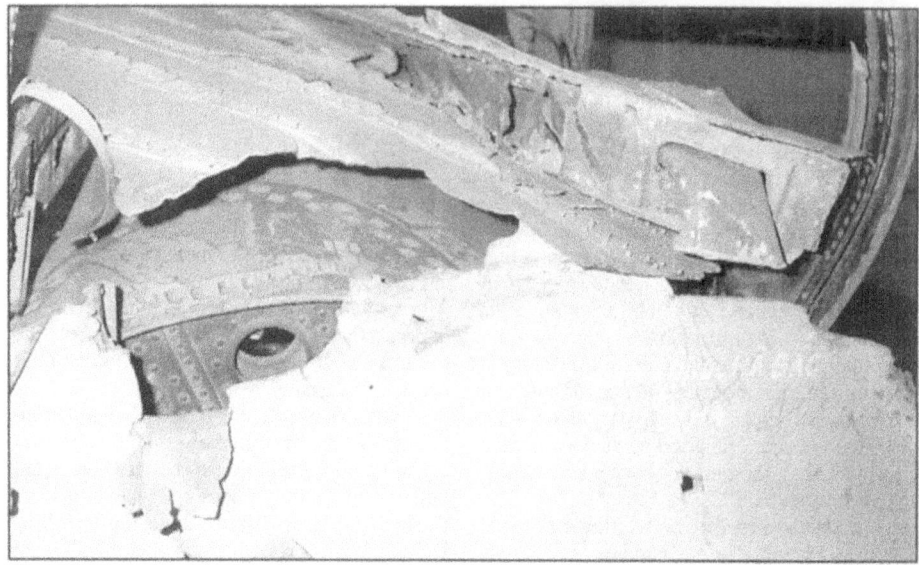

This photo was taken at the Vietnamese AF Museum, Hanoi 1995-96. It shows wreckage from an F-4 shot down on 12-9-72. Courtesy of George Petersen.

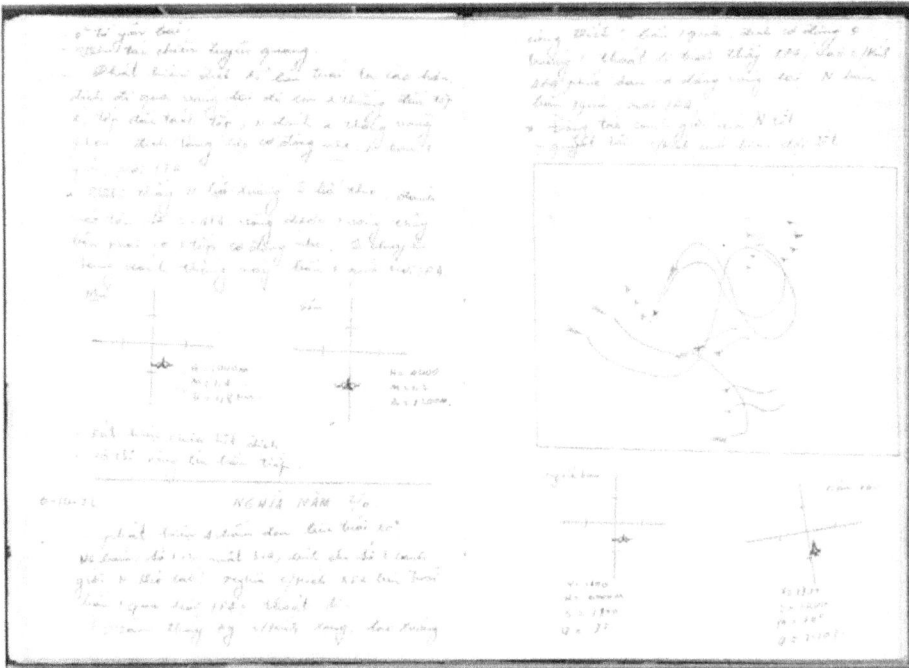
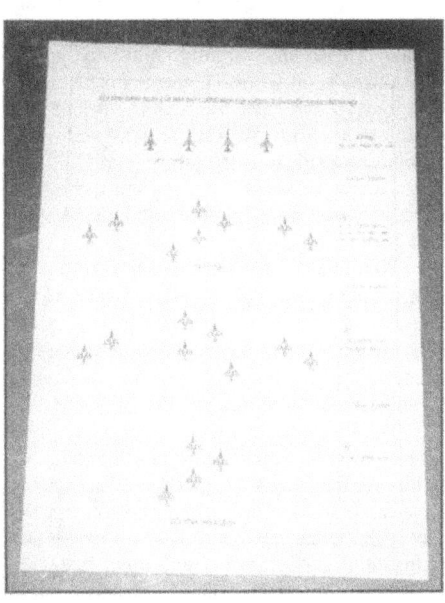

Wartime NVA-USAF F4 formation info from "B-52" museum, Hanoi 1998. Courtesy of George Petersen.

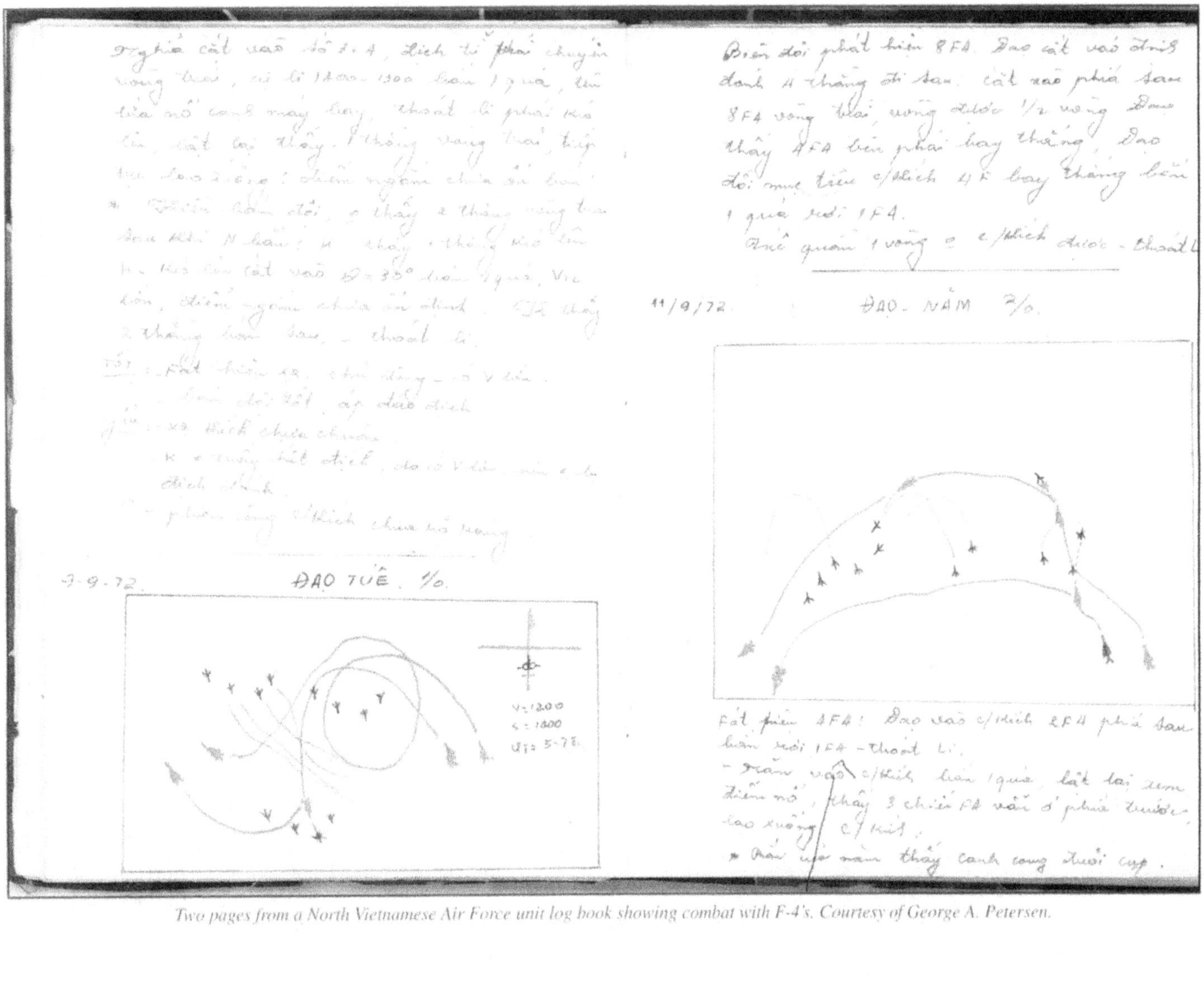

Two pages from a North Vietnamese Air Force unit log book showing combat with F-4's. Courtesy of George A. Petersen.

have to make at least two passes per aircraft; things were going well and we were unscathed until I made my last pass and pickled my remaining bombs on the target. As I pulled off the target clawing for altitude, there was a humongous flash and loud noise slightly below and just in front of my right wing. The force of the explosion was so hard that the whole airplane just shuddered while my RIO and myself were thrown from side to side in the cockpit.

I knew we were in deep yogurt, the only question was if the aircraft would hold together long enough for us to get over water.

Your chances for survival and rescue were much better if you could eject over water. Coming down over land could result in your being shot up while hanging from the parachute or executed on the ground by some p.o.'d villagers for messing up their rice paddies.

The F-4 has a tele-light panel on the right side of the instrument panel that contains 42 lights which give you a general system status of the aircraft, kind of like idiot lights in a car. Directly above the tele-panel is a master caution light, "think about leaving" and above that is the master warning light, "major problems, might be flyable, leave now."

From the corner of my eye, I could see the tele-panel twinkling like a freaking Christmas tree which was not a good sign. PC1, my number one hydraulic system was rapidly unwinding to less than 2000 PSI, normal is 2750. Number two engine's EPR was dropping along with the EGT. At this point there was no doubt in my mind that my RIO and I would be going for a swim very soon.

We had about 10 miles to go to get over water so I selected full afterburner, only to be rewarded with a chug (unstart) on No. 2. The engine promptly pooled down and took the CSD off-line with it.

My RIO called out the shut down procedures as I secured the engine, I looked outside the cockpit and saw the inlet ramps fluttering back and forth. No. 5 LE slat was completely gone, No. 4 had been substantially damaged and there were numerous black marks on the BLC tubes and top of the wing. In addition, the flak burst had apparently substantially holed No. 2 intake as there were several holes that I could see through.

After securing the fuel and ignition, I set-up the aircraft for best flight with battle damage and asymmetrical thrust with No. 2 engine shut down.

As we crabbed for the North Vietnam coastline, I keyed my RIO and asked him if he was ready to go. He keyed the mike once (yes), that was all I needed for him to do at this point. I reached over and moved the ejection sequence handle to command, rear. This would ensure that the would eject first and that I would follow him out of the airplane.

The tele-panel lights continued to twinkle on and off; then I saw the master caution light glow momentarily and go out, another bad sign, the aircraft continued to shed parts, I had the rudder almost hard over to the left, the drag from the airframe damage made it difficult to fly as we headed for the coast.

As we reached water, I looked down and saw that PC1 was at 0 and PC2 was bounding off the accumulator at about 1000 PSI. I thought I saw the master warning light come on and figuring that we couldn't get much further, I hit the emergency vent button to dump cockpit pressurization then keyed the mike and said the magic word, "eject, eject, eject." A micro second later the AFT canopy blew off with a loud bang and a thud and my RIO departed the airplane. Another micro second passed, I blew my canopy off, reached up and grabbed the face curtain and departed my crippled aircraft.

I saw that Coop had been able to head father into the Gulf and I was hoping that both of our PRC-10s (rescue radios) were working. As I got close to the water, I tried to recall all the training we had been given then realized that I hadn't released my seat pan yet. The seat pan is on the end of 25 foot lanyard and contains survival goodies and your life raft. When the seat pan is deployed, it deploys and inflates your life raft and helps you to judge when you are about to enter the water.

When my seat pan hit the water, I reached up and popped my Koch fittings so that I wouldn't get entangled in the shroud lines, and found myself swimming in the Tonkin Gulf. While retrieving the lanyard, I extracted my radio and started to transmit only to find that Coop had been able to get right through to our rescue guys.

About 30 minutes later, a Kaman Seasprite from the boat appeared and dropped a PJ in the water with Coop. Subsequently, the chopper located me and I clipped my D-ring on my torso harness to the chopper's rescue rig and was winched aboard.

We were recovered aboard the *Kitty Hawk* between launches and as we landed, many flight deck crew members were yelling and waving. It sure felt good to be "home" again.

We owed it all to the rescue crew from HC-1, Det. Charlie.

When the boat pulled into Yokosuka, Japan a couple of weeks later, Coop and I went to the base exchange and bought both the parachute riggers a bottle of scotch; the helicopter crew asked for and received a mixed case of booze, price $55.00. It was little price to pay for packing good chutes and saving our lives.

FLYING IN THE PHANTOM AS A PHOTOJOURNALIST
by Don Spering, AIR

I saw my first F-4 Phantom at Andrews AFB, MD in the mid 1960s and became very impressed with her overall size and appearance. I had been a real fan of the Republic F-105 Thud. The Thud had flown right my backyard, McGuire AFB, NJ. The runway approach was just beyond my house.

My first jet fighter ride was in a F-106B Delta Dart, soon to follow the Thud. The Phantom was starting to become the replacement jet fighter for most units that had been flying F-100s

and F-105s. My contacts from previous photo flights with many units helped me get started on my goal to have 100 flight hours in the Phantom, a goal I obtained in 1992, thanks to the Birmingham ANG; not bad for a civilian with no military time.

My first Phantom ride was with the 117 TRW at Birmingham, AL. I remember the overwhelming power and brute force that was involved in getting the F-4 into the air. You would taxi to the end of the runway, make last minute checks and then get kicked in the pants as the two J-79 torched off and hurled you down the runway and into the air. The wheels came up and you were passing 200 knots and heading for the blue. I knew then and there that I was falling in love with the beast and wanted to get as many rides as I could and take as many pictures of the Phantom in flight.

I had over a hundred sorties, dropping bombs, flares and taking recon photos. Did AMC, DACT, air combat, refueling, went straight up and straight down, turned, banked and rolled the Phantom myself. All this time having four cameras with me in the backpit.

Taking pictures from the backseat was no easy task. You sat in the pit and had to be aware of the canopy glares and not to shoot through the lower part of the canopies close to the rails where there was to much distortion. The biggest problem was getting the camera close to your face so you could focus the lens. I used two Nikon F3 with sports finders that allowed me to get a better view through the lens without my oxygen mask causing too much of a problem. You couldn't run the seat all the way up, especially being six foot tall. Too far up and close to the canopies would cause your head to bang off the canopy as you banked and rolled from side to side. Changing film was never a real problem. I just had to remember not to do it during a pull-up maneuver and get caught with my head down while pulling 4-5Gs. It was almost impossible to get your head back up until after the unloading of the G-forces and besides, it hurts. I would shoot on average 18 to 20 rolls of film on each sortie, color and b/w. Never took film canisters with me. I would load the film into my right leg G-suit pocket and place the exposed film as I changed it into my left leg G-suit pocket. I would take along two helmet bags, one with my camera gear and one with my helmet. As I unloaded the bags I would lay one on each side in the cockpit covering the instrument panels and placing some of my gear on top of the bags. Most of the time this was fine until I had to use the radio or instruments during the flight. I would try to watch it on the radar to keep my bearings about me. It never seemed easy, as I always had to much gear and always trying to keep my head up and see everything that was happening, always looking for the next shot. I enjoyed the formations and the turns, as there was always something in he view finder to shoot. My trademark was the vertical. During mission planning I would always brief the vertical shot and how I wanted to achieve it. I usually asked for a loop, starting out in level flight and getting spacing and location between the aircraft. We would start 3-4G pull at 320-350 knots, sometimes 00 knots. We would head straight up, over the top and down the backside. All the time shooting pictures and swapping cameras. Our aircraft would take the lead so I was always looking back as we passed through the vertical. This allowed the horizon to appear in the photo and showed the angle of the flight. The real trick was getting our aircraft to maneuver line abreast to slightly behind our wingman, allowing me to still have the horizon in the viewfinder of my camera.

Some of the best photography was accomplished on an up and down spiral. We would start at about 6,000 feet, get up to 20,000 and then down to 6,000 again. All the time we would fly the wingman position which allowed me to have the lead Phantom in front of the camera all the time. The end results were very impressive, creating spectacular photos.

I am fortunate to have been allowed to fly for the past 25 years. I must state that I can take the photo, but it is the pilot and his skills that really allow me to get the superb shots. Their flying abilities get the aircraft in close, far enough forward or at the right altitude. To them and especially the Phantom drivers, I enjoyed every flight I had. I ended up with about 130 hours in the "pit" of the Phantom and had McDonnell-Douglas issue me a 100 plus certificate. Phantoms Phorever.

PUNCH OUT
By Wayne Smith

Egress is not noticed on a day to day basis, but one that determines life or death when put to use.

Take a warm Monday afternoon in July 1979, just before the 1630 shift change. I was walking through the parking lot toward the Egress Shop when I stopped to watch a pair of F-4Es that had just took off.

I noticed something horribly wrong. The left wing tip on one F-4 had folded up a 90 degree angle with the jet headed towards the Phase Inspection hangers. The stricken Phantom managed to just clear the hangers when time shifted into slow motion.

Overhead, two small pieces of something clear flew away from top of one of the aircraft just milliseconds later, two small flames of orange/red appeared above and behind the F-4. The crew had punched out. Ejection took place at around 400 feet altitude.

Time seemed to speed up back to normal as I watched the aircraft roll over, belly up and headed back towards the earth and the direction of the base fuel storage tanks.

Within five or six seconds, the dull impact and explosion was heard and then the all too familiar orange and black cloud was seen. By now the sirens of emergency vehicles headed towards the crash site were evident.

As I turned my attention back to the drama unfolding above my head, the crew had full parachutes and were descending towards the flight line.

The ejection seats, on the other hand, were coming down a little ahead of me in the parking lot. The forward seat impacted upon the concrete lot and bounced twice, buckling up like a can being stepped upon.

The aft seat came down right on top a van that was parked and then came to rest upright behind the vehicle. By looking at the seat, one wouldn't think it was involved in a ejection.

I believe the fire had been brought under control in 20 minutes or so. Later, I was informed that the F-4 had indeed impacted just 100 yards from the fuel storage area. A disaster that was 300 feet away.

The pilot was praised for his control of the jet and veering away from the fuel storage area

Van hit by AFT ejection seat, F4E 69-7269. Courtesy of Wayne Smith.

F-4E 69-7269 after crash. Courtesy of Wayne Smith.

RF-4C 'BH' 65-0867 'Phirst in Phantoms' 'Birmingham Belle' 'Jed's Jet' 106 RS/117 RW, Birmingham Arpt, Ala-Ang. Apr-94 CW photo: Don Spearing/AIR.

before ejection. Crew members were Capt. Glen R. McConnell and 2nd Lt. Howard B. Ruth in the 69-7269 F-4E. Both crew members returned to flying status after a few days.

MY LIFE WITH THE F-4
by Roland D. Hamblin

I became aware of the F-4 during the early 1970s when I was at school. I would see them flying fairly low over the fields beyond our sports field, presumably either out of Wethersfield (which was very near my school), Lakenheath, Alconbury or Bentwaters/Woodbridge. A couple of years later, while on a family holiday to Cornwall, we stopped at RNAS Yeovilton to visit the RNAS Museum. While there, I spotted several RN Phantoms sporting Jubilee markings (the year was 1977, the Queen's Jubilee year). That was what got me finally hooked. The father of one of my friends worked at a local electronics firm, which was involved with the RN/RAF F-4 radar and he sportingly provided me with a side view drawing (all three feet of it), which is now one of my prized possessions. From then on, it was no holes barred. The F-4, for me, was "the aircraft." A visit to RAF Greenham Common IAT 1979 brought an encounter with the specially painted Alcock and Brown RAF F-4M, along with my first Spanish F-4. Regular visits to the annual Mildenhall airshow from 1981 (except for 1991, when my son was born and 1999 due to the show being canceled) and the IAT sporadically during the 1980s due to getting married (although my wife was very tolerant) and moving to the Netherlands for three years and regularly during the 1990s (only missed 1990) brought Turkish, Spanish and German; RNAS Yeovilton in June 1994 brought Greek and RAF Lakenheath during the mid 1990s brought Egyptian F-4s into my log book.

During the early 1990s, I saw the phasing out of the F-4 from RAF service (it had been phased out of RN service a few years earlier). During 1990 and 1991, RAF Wattisham became a pilgrimage location for me, as that was where RAF Phantom's "went to die." I remember going to the Phantom Meet in 1990 thinking, "how much longer can this last?" It was only to last one more year. On Sept. 30, 1991, I saw the official disbandment of 74th Sqdn. with a flypast taking place Oct. 1. I am rather fortunate to be able to say I was there, albeit watching from the public side of one of the crash gates. It was great to see the crews waving as they taxied past, followed by multi-ship take-offs and a nine ship flypast. I have not seen anything as spectacular by the F-4 since (yet).

With all the scrapping taking place in the UK, where could I go to see my beloved F-4? The Battle of Britain display at RAF Leuchars in 1993 was a good place to start. Black Mike from 111th Sqdn. was allowing cockpit photos, so guess who was one of the first in the queue (thanks to my two mates goading me on). To be sitting in the front cockpit was rather spectacular, even if it was on the ground. I had previously sat in the rear cockpit of one of the first RN F-4s at the RNAS Museum Yeovilton in April 1991.

Where could I go now? Fortunately, after a couple of job changes, I was presented with probably the best opportunity I have had to hunt the F-4. I am now working for a computer services company, involved with an aircraft weight and balance system. This system was part of the overall change of reservations system being installed in the United Kingdom's second largest airline and one of the key people involved in the installation lived in Tucson, AZ, just around the corner from AMARC. My boss, a friend and I went on tour in Tucson in November 1998, flying over the base for 50 minutes (spending quite a lot of time over the F-4s) and crawling the wire, taking photos, logging serials and generally having a good time (especially me, logging around 150 F-4s from the fence alone). Tail codes that seemed never to be seen were suddenly all around me. From AMARC, we went to Pima and I now have a framed photo of me standing with my arm on the nose cone of 66-0329/ED. Pure heaven.

And it did not end there. From Tucson, we flew into Los Angeles and drove up to Mojave for a ramp tour. Guess what was on the ramp, more F-4s (then Tracor Flight Systems, now Bae Systems). In total, I logged around 25 F-4s at

Mojave, plus four at Pima, a couple of hundred at AMARC and a few bits in the scrapyards surrounding AMARC. My wife thought that I would finally get it out of my system, but she says that I have been worse since my return.

Since then, my log rate for the F-4 has tailed off somewhat, but I am hopeful that one day, I will get to Greece, Turkey, Spain and Germany, log as many F-4s as possible and not get arrested.

Israel, Egypt, Korea and Japan will have to wait for now.

Where finances permit, I purchase every book on the F-4 and my collection now numbers around 80 titles. Plastic kits are also an obsession (or at least were, until the children arrived). I have models ranging from 1:44 to 1:32 and most scales in between. These are all unmade and awaiting my retirement, when I can dig out my numerous photos, peruse my books and remember "they don't make aircraft like that anymore." My best friend thinks I am a tad obsessive (he prefers the F-15) but I feel I am justified, don't you?

A CREW CHIEF AND HIS PHANTOM'S FINAL HOURS
by Don Spering, AIR

During the early 1990s I spent a lot of time at Birmingham, AL flying in their Phantoms and painting their jets. As 1994 rolled around, the Phantoms from Birmingham started to be phased out and sent to Davis-Monthan AFB, AZ for storage. One of the many friends I made at the 117TRW was crew chief Jed Dailey and his assigned jet "867". Jed had commented on numerous occasions that his Phantom was in need of an overall paint scheme and due the phase-out that would never happen.

I proceeded to apply colorful artwork to Jed's jet during its last week at Birmingham. The day prior to his pride, joy and love left for Davis-Monthan AFB and eventual use as a drone, Jed's emotions were evident. Jed tinkered with his jet throughout the morning as I applied some artwork. Even though the Phantom didn't have a shiny new paint scheme Jed kept babying his Phantom, cleaning it, wiping it down with care and knowing that time was getting short for 867 on Birmingham ramp. The thoughts of his Phantom taking off for the last time were really starting to play on his mind and I could see that the reality was starting to come into focus. His comments and his manner of work reflected his forthcoming final hour. It was breaktime and Jed said, "Don, I'll be back in about 10 minutes or so." The tone of his voice echoed his reluctance to leave his jet.

The 10 minutes went by quite fast for Jed, he eagerly returned to his Phantom on the line and he handed me a piece of paper. I put my paint brush down and read the following:

Reconnaissance ex-Luftwaffe Phantom 7500 in Italy during August 1994. The former Luftwaffe scheme was maintained by Greece. Photo Sergio Botaro via Martin Collection.

RF-4C at Hill AFB for depot repair on return from SEA assigned 11 TRS 432 TRW on September 18, 1973. Photo Ben Knowles via Martin Collection.

Luke based F-4C Phantom from the 311 TFTS 58 TFTW displays the early tactical scheme. Photo: Martin Collection.

Here rests a great jet,
Twenty-four years a crew chief's pet.
Though I only crewed the last three years,
The day it left I shed a few tears.
Three decades of blood, tears and sweat,
And it's still the prettiest and fastest jet.
Countless hours of phases and inspections,
From civilians and all maintenance sections.
Now on to bigger and better things,
And maybe someday we'll again hear these engines sing.
May the spirit of flight be with our jets and all crews,
For the Lord knows together we've paid our dues. by Jed Daily, 867 Crew Chief, April 1994.

As I read the poem Jed gave me, a tear came to my eye. Jed placed a copy in the forms book that was sent aloft on that final flight for someone at the other end to read and know this Phantom had a friend indeed. Yes, those at Birmingham had lots of fond and lasting memories which will be with them for many years to come and for some it will always be "Phantoms Phorever."

Spanish reconnaissance Phantom CR.12-57 seen in Italy during 1996. Spain was one of three southern European Phantom users. Photo: Martin Collection.

29 April 85, 64-1033. (P) Capt. Causey with Capt. Grand. Courtesy M. Holloway.

Capt Baxley, SRA Mike Hall, F-4G 69-0244, June 91. Courtesy of M.R. Hall.

RAF Phantom FG.1 Treble-One squadron all black special XV582 taxies in following a display at RAF Brawdy in August 1990.

(L to R) LTC Bob 'Push' Pardo, Col. Steve Ritchie (Ace Vietnam conflict), Gen James Renschen (131 TFW CMDR MO-ANG) and LTC Jeffery Fienstein (Ace Vietnam Conflict) during Phantom Farewell activities hosted by the 131 TFW MO-ANG, September 91 at St. Louis, MO. Photo by Don Spering/AIR.

FOR SALE

1 RF4C

NEEDS WORK

~~$250,000 Firm~~
~~$1,000,000~~
$500.00 O.B.O

ACFT- of the Nevada Air National Guard 1995. Sign in camera window just before departure to AMARC- Aircraft. 64-1030 or (Dirty 30). Crew Chief TSGT Mike Andrews. Courtesy of R.G. Langley.

Photo credit Soner Capoglu.

Photo Gallery of the F-4 Phantom II

Colorful markings were a hallmark of USN Phantom for many years. This Ardvard VF-114 F-4J awaits use at NAS Miramar in June 1973. Photo Clive Moggridge via Martin Collection.

There were only two examples of the EF-4B and both were assigned to VAQ-33. Photo Terry Waddington via Martin Collection.

Courtesy of Charles Weiss.

This USN drone taxies back in after a display at the 2000 Phancon. Photo courtesy of Steve Wilcox.

Photo credit Soner Capoglu.

Courtesy of M.R. Hall.

Taken at NAF Atsugi on 1 Nov 1970. 151006 NF-102 VF-161. Courtesy of Arika Watanabe.

Taken at Iwakuni in November 1976. 153828 VE-000 VMFA-115 Photo by Akira Watanabe.

RF4C's of the Nevada Air National Guard. Courtesy of R.G. Langley.

June 1969, 67-0338 F-4E, Bullpups Danang run. Courtesy of D.R Kuntz.

F4E before being painted in T-Bird Scheme, August 1996, A/C# 60284, 6510 Test Wing, Edwards Air Force Base, CA. Courtesy of W. Smith.

Taken at Yokota Air Base on 20 March 1970. 80 TFS 347 TFW. Courtesy of Akira Watanabe.

Taken at Yokota Air Base in 1970. 559 TFS 12 TFW. Courtesy of Akira Watanabe.

Spanish F-4C's, all ex-USAF aircraft, were maintained in USAF early camouflage as shown by these three aircraft. Photo: Martin Collection.

This F-4F Phantom rides high above the cloud base on patrol. Photo: Martin Collection.

This 1988 shot shows the larger style markings used by early German Phantoms. This Phantom is painted in the early splinter scheme with a non-standard tail. Photo: Martin Collection.

Holloman, New Mexico based German Phantoms were painted and marked as per USAF examples. The give-a-way was the German flag color on the fin cap and the 1975 serial for this F-4E. These F-4E's were manufactured for use in the USA based training unit. Photo: Martin Collection.

This 111 Squadron Phantom approaches the runway threshold after a spirited display at RNAS Culdrose in 1983. Photo courtesy of Patrick Martin.

69-0245. Courtesy of M.R. Hall.

Courtesy of C.W. Basso.

Courtesy of C.W. Basso.

Taken at Yokota Air Base on 3 July 1970, 155815 VMFA-334. Courtesy of Akira Watanabe.

Taken at Yokota Air Base on 8 January 1972, 153108 VMCJ-1. Courtesy of Akira Watanabe.

St. Louis Phantoms, the tail of the 30th Anniversary Phantom from the 131 TFW, May 1988. Courtesy of Don Spering/AIR.

Amarc (Bone Yard) bound, RF4C's of the Nevada Air National Guard. Courtesy of R.G. Langley.

Courtesy of L.K. McClung.

This 56 Squadron Phantom FGR.2 performs a high-speed pass at RAF Coningsby just prior to phase-out and replacement by the Tornado F.2 and F.3. Photo courtesy of R. Daniels.

A sight not often seen, a mass flyby of Phantoms. Photo courtesy of R. Daniels.

28 August 1982, RF-4C 64-1056 117 TRW/106 TRS, Birmingham ANG Base, AL. Ground crew parking and choking aircraft. Courtesy of Mike Holloway.

This F-4C carries the markings of the LA-ANG stationed at NAS New Orleans, the 'Coonass Militia.' The 122 TFS/159 TFG flew the Phantom from 1979 to 1985 when they converted and became the first ANG Unit to fly the McDonnell-Douglas F-15 Eagle. Courtesy of Don Spering/AIR.

Spring 1966. F4G Buno 150484. Squadron VF-213 BlackLions. USS Kitty Hawk CVA-63. Courtesy of Val Valentine.

F-4E 335 TFW at Maple Flag in May 1985. Photo courtesy of Patrick Martin.

F-4E of the Thunderbirds at Davis-Monthan AFB in March 1972. Photo: Martin Collection.

Taken at Yokota Air Base, Japan on 9 March 1970. GG:35TFS 347TFW; GR: 80TFS 347TFW. Courtesy of Akira Watanabe.

The 141 TFS/108 TFW, NJ-ANG McGuire AFB, NJ holds the record for the amount of sorties generated during a one day surge. 127 sorties completed to the gunnery range out of 128 phantoms launched on November 3, 1990. Courtesy of Don Spering/AIR.

A former F-4G converted to drone QF-4G awaits use at Tyndall AFB. High-visibility markings and various modified "bumps". Photo courtesy of Steve Wilcox.

The all blue special for 92 Squadron RAF was displayed at the 1991 IAT at RAF Fairford. Photo courtesy of Patrick Martin.

Following completion of service, Phantoms of all US services were stored at AMARC, located adjacent to Davis-Monthan AB. Many were to fly again in Navy and Air Force drone programs. Photo courtesy of Michael Head.

13 April 94, flight line at Birmingham ANG Base during last days of RF-4C operations. Courtesy of Mike Holloway.

The AKG52 reconnaissance Phantom displays the early splinter scheme used on all 88 RF-4E. Photo courtesy of Hans Schroder via Martin Collection.

North Dakota ANG used the Happy Hooligans in a red band as their squadron markings. The unit was also quick to apply these markings to some visiting aircraft. Photo: Martin Collection.

Courtesy of C.W. Basso.

The only F-4G assigned to the 152 RS, Nevada Air National Guard. Courtesy of R.G. Langley.

For the 2000 Maple Flag exercise the Luftwaffe sent a composite group from several wings to CFB Cold Lake. Photo courtesy of Patrick Martin.

Participating in the June 1985 Red Flag exercise, was F-4G Phantom 69-246 from the 562 TFTS 27 TFW based at George AFB. Photo courtesy of Patrick Martin.

This Texas ANG F-4C Phantom adds a splash of color to the air defense scheme in June 1984. Photo courtesy of Charles Mayer.

Until the advent of the ADC grey scheme, guard and reserve Phantoms used the standard tactical camouflage scheme. The Hawaii ANG displays this scheme in November 1984. Photo courtesy of Daniel Soulaine.

Biographies of the F-4 Phantom II Society

184th TFG air crew members pose for the camera at Davis-Monthan AFB, Arizona after completing their last flight in the F4D. Courtesy of Don Spering/AIR.

CHARLES W. ARRINGTON, has been a lifelong Kentuckian. He received a bachelor's degree from the University of Louisville and a master's from Western Kentucky University. Since retiring as a middle school teacher, Charlie has been researching the history of aviation in Louisville and writing a series of articles on the subject.

Charlie traces his interest in aviation to building plastic models as a youngster. He became a Phantom Phan (sic) after seeing his first one in 1967 and knew that he was hooked when he saw the Thunderbirds perform in 1971. Phantoms became a common sight in Louisville in 1976 when the Kentucky Air National Guard converted to the RF-4C. Charlie spent the next 13 years photographing the various paint schemes and marking changes on KYANG Phantoms. In 1987, he had the ultimate Phantom thrill with an orientation ride, courtesy of the Kentucky Air National Guard.

DAVID W. AUNGST, born April 3, 1962 and lives in Pottstown, PA. He didn't serve with any units because he was disqualified because of bee sting allergy, but he is an interested bystander.

He remembers sharing his first time on an active flightline with the society and F-4s at Phan-Con 91 in St. Louis.

He is a computer programmer and a published author in fine scale *Modeler Magazine* and *Smoke Trails*. David and wife Renee have two children, Christopher and Alexander.

STEPHEN J. "BARNEY" BARNSHAW, born Dec. 13, 1953 in Fort Lee, VA and currently lives in Fayetteville, GA. Trained at Lowry Technical Training Center, Lowry AFB, CO, October 1971 to July 1972 and Pittsburgh Institute of Aeronautics, March 1973 to January 1978.

Units served with include 6585th Test Group, AF Systems Command, Holloman AFB, NM (Central Inertial Guidance Test Facility), July 1972 to September 1975.

Discharged with the rank of sergeant in 1975. His awards include the AFOUA, AFGCM, NDSM and SAEMR.

Memorable Experiences: the sights and sounds of F-4s were nearly an everyday experience as Holloman was home to four squads of F-4Ds (49th TFW, TAC); witnessed successful ejection by Thunderbird RT Wingman after collision with leader F-4 in diamond formation take-off at base air show, March 1973. The remaining three aircraft landed safely.

For the past 20 years he has been an aircraft maintenance tech with Delta Air Lines, Atlanta, GA.

Significant Achievements: has a private pilot's license (April 1974); advanced open water diver; with a co-worker completely rebuilt entire empennage (excluding fabric control surfaces), left wing and both wing tips of Delta Air Transport Heritage Museum's DC-3, Ship 41 (to be air worthy).

CLIFFORD U. BASSO, born in Raleigh, NC. Served from December 1968 to December 1978 and attained the rank of E-5. He trained at Millington, TN and Oceana, VA; served with VF-41.

Memorable Experiences: serving under CDR Cane; photos from every angle of F-4 on the USS *Roosevelt* (CVA-42).

He is a computer and telephone tech and lives in Old Hickory, TN with his wife. They have a son and daughter.

ROBERT L. "BOB" BECKMAN, born May 28, 1953, Highland Park, IL. Joined the service in September 1972; trained at Sheppard AFB, TX; stationed at Kunsan AB, ROK.

Served with 3rd TFW, 8th TFW, 432nd TFW, 388th TFW, 49th FIS, 4713th DSES, 86th TFW, 56th TFW, 64th FTW and 51st TFW.

Memorable Experiences: his aircraft F-4E 68-0412, no delayed discrepancies on a black letter initial.

Discharged in April 1994 as E-7. Awards include two MSM, three AF Commendations and AF Achievement.

Achievements: Crew Chief of the Month, Senior NCO of the Month, Excellent Engine Bay Insp. for F-4s.

Currently HVAC tech, engineering student in college. Divorced, he has two sons living with him in Wildwood, IL.

EILEEN BJORKMAN, LTC, born in Texas, but as an Air Force brat, grew up all over the US. After graduating from the University of Washington in 1979, she worked for a year, then joined the Air Force, earning a commission through OTS in August 1980.

She spent two years at Holloman AFB testing inertial navigation systems; in 1984, she was selected for the USAF Test Pilot School (TPS) at Edwards AFB as a flight test engineer. For four years, she flew in the F-4, first as a TPS student, then at the F-16 Combined Test Force and then as a TPS instructor. Despite having flown over 25 different airplanes, including all the "teenager" fighters, the F-4 is her favorite.

Between 1995 and 1998, she was again stationed at Holloman AFB, which renewed her interest in the F-4. She is still on active duty and currently stationed at Eglin AFB.

GORDON M. "SLATS" BOOTH, LTCDR, born Sept. 4, 1945, Cheshire, United Kingdom. He served in the military from 1967 to 1975.

Trained at Linton-on-ouse, Leuchars Yeovilton, 1967-69. Served with Fleet Air Arm: 700P SQN, IFTU, 767 SQN, 892 SQN.

He remembers the first launch and recovery being incredible.

Currently he is general manager of International Food Ingredients. He considers himself the world wide society recruiter.

Married to Marilyn, he has a son, Duncan and daughter, Helen.

GLENN EDWARD "ED" BOWERS,

born Dec. 28, 1953 in Nashville, TN and grew up with a love of locomotives. After graduating from Belmont College, he somehow ended up in the Navy as a RAN in RA-5C Vigilantes (1977-79) and was fortunate to make the last cruise in RVAH-7. From there he went to a three year exchange tour with the USAF at Bergstrom AFB, TX in RF-4C Phantoms. About the time he was given RIO orders to F-14 Tomcats, the Reserves at Bergstrom traded in their C-130's for a more manly aircraft, the F-4D Phantom. Ed moved there instead and was quite fortunate in flying the D until 1989 and the TISEO E until July 1991 when he made his last Phantom flight to AMARC. Before retiring in 1997, he was able to fly both in the F-15 and F-16, but misses the Phantom the most.

He has over 1500 hours in the Phantom, 500 in the Vigilante and flights in many other USN and USAF aircraft.

Ed just completed his 10th year with Lockheed Martin supporting NASA at Johnson Space Center. He spent close to three years in Moscow while working the NASA/Mir program and while there, was able to meet many Cosmonauts. In addition, with the help of a former Buran Cosmonaut, was able to not only visit the Russian Aviation Museum at Monina, but two visits to Zhukovsky Airbase where he obtained many excellent photos to add to his large aviation collection that continues to gather dust due to lack of time.

Since retirement from the Reserves, Ed has spent time enlarging his locomotive leasing firm and now owns 15 diesel-electric locomotives and one private car. Recently married to the former Svetlana Victorovna Kurlykina of Moscow, Russia, Ed is also busy with family life. He has also been asked recently to supply slides for upcoming publications in both the aviation and railroad hobby areas.

CURTIS M. "CURT" BURNS, born

June 15, 1931 in Bryan, TX. Commissioned 2nd lieutenant on graduation from Texas A&M and ordered to active duty in 1952. Flying training at Bartow and Bryan, graduated in 1954. Flew F-86E/Fs at Nellis and Williams, then F-100Cs in the 53rd FDS/TFS at Landstuhl AB, Germany. Group flying safety officer at Aviano AB, Italy flying F-IOODs with TAC Rotation Squadrons. Flight commander and ops officer in a MAP Plt. Training Sqd. that taught students from 26 nations to fly at Moody and then Randolph AFBs. Armed Forces Staff College at Norfolk, then F-4C, RTU at Davis Monthan AFB. Flew F-4Cs in the 559th TFS at Cam Ranh Bay and finished the RVN tour as in-country briefing officer for Gen. Brown at 7th AF. Flew 19 combat sorties in the F-5 with the VNAF. Subsequent tour as Chief of Flight Safety, then Director of Safety, 17th AF, Ramstein AB. Attached to 32nd TFS at Soesterberg to fly the F-4E. Last assignment before retiring in 1973 was as Director of Safety, 52nd TFW, Spangdahlem AB.

Joined College of Business Administration faculty at Texas A&M University and retired again in 1986. Now active in aviation history organizations and flying his antique Culver V.

Achievements: served his country, had a hell of a lot of fun flying the fabulous fighters of the 50s and 60s and still married after 48 years to his wonderful wife, Ann.

HENRY BUSCH, born and raised on

Long Island, NY about three miles from Republic Aviation Corporation where his dad worked. As a youngster growing up he took many trips with his mom over to pick up his dad at work. There he would spend many hours watching the F-84s and then the F-105s. He remembers the Thud most of all so it is obvious that his first aviation love was the F-105.

During his teen years as the flying activities at RAC dwindled his aviation enthusiasm became focused on the next best thing for a while, cars. Modeling was another of his hobbies. Mostly cars but an occasional jet would be in there. Airplanes were still on his mind but not as prevalent. Henry got married in 1967 and in 1969 moved his family up to the Catskill Mountains of New York where there isn't any close military aviation. The closest military base is at least three hours away.

When his dad passed away in 1975 he acquired some of the things his dad collected during his 38 years of employment with Republic. As he was going through some of this stuff he started reading stories about the F-105 in SEA. That got the aviation enthusiasm going again. He started his aviation book collection with anything about the Air War in SEA. He learned more about the F-105 and the other workhorse of the war, the F-4 Phantom II. He has extended his book collection to include reference material on most of today's military aviation. While he claims to have every book on the F-105, his F-4 Phantom collection isn't complete yet.

Henry is an avid modeler building museum quality models. He likes to refer to them as "replicas." "Building a museum quality replica is an art. Not just putting a kit together. Not everyone can do it." Although he can build anything, he prefers military jets. He has an extensive collection of replicas of which the majority is Phantoms naturally. Photography is another hobby that he enjoys and extended it to his love of aviation. His photo collection numbers in the thousands. He has had the opportunity to do some air to air photography a number of times thanks to his good friend Don Spering of AIR.

Henry has been working for the Sullivan County DPW since 1969 when he started as a parts clerk. He is presently their fleet maintenance manager responsible for the maintenance and operation of 700 plus pieces of equipment and the logistics and support for the entire department.

While visiting the Air Force Museum in 1988 he came upon an issue of *Smoke Trails*. He immediately filled out the membership application to join the Phantom Society. He has attended every Phan Con since. He even took his wife to a couple. She loved it, by the way.

SONER CAPOGLU, born July 20, 1964

in Eskisehir, Turkey and devoted himself more than 10 years to making the aerial photographs.

So far he has flown with many kinds of jet fighter/trainer aircrafts like F-5B, NF-

5B, CF-104D, F-4E, F-16D, T-33A, T-37B/C, T-38A, etc. His photographs have appeared in local and international journals and magazines.

His photos have been published in the Turkish Air Force Official wall calendars, 1991 through 1998 and in many other firm calendars as well.

His works have been awarded and made him to take place among the best aviation photographers in the world.

ER-NING CHANG, born May 25, 1951 at Taipei, Taiwan. He is an independent consultant on computer programming.

Currently residing in Dublin, OH, he is married with one daughter.

CHARLES GORDON "CAJUN" CLOUTIER JR., Major, grew up in Shreveport, LA watching the P-38s and B-25 pilots train for WWII and knew that flying was in his future. He graduated from La Tech with a mechanical engineering degree and 2nd lieutenant commission in the USAF.

Pilot training was completed in the T-34 and T-28 at Maldin AB, MO, then T-33s at Vance AFB, OK. After flying medium range B-47 bombers in the SAC for seven years (ugh) he returned to Vance AFB as a T-37 instructor pilot in the Undergraduate Pilot Training Program. After this tour he finally got to fly the airplane of his dreams, the F-4 Phantom. He was assigned to Davis-Monthan AFB, AZ for what was to become his most memorable and exciting tour of his Air Force career. Then more good fortune came February 1971 with an assignment to Udorn Royal Thai AB in Thailand with the famed 555TFS, Triple Nickel. The missions were always exciting because they varied so

much. Not only did he fly MiG Cap for search and rescue (SAR), but dropped many types of ordinance such as 500 pound bombs, 2,000 pound laser guided bombs, CBUs, white phosphorus and napalm to name a few. With the "pucker factor" going up and 207 missions, it was time to return the good ole USA.

He was awarded the DFC w/OLC, Air Medal w/14 OLCs and RVN Campaign Medal among his numerous other decorations. Gordon retired from the Air Force in 1979 at Barksdale AFB, LA. He and his wife, Paulette, are currently enjoying fishing and life on the beach in Gulf Shores, AL.

ROYCE "ROY" G. COLDING, Ret, USAF, MSgt, born 1936 in Plant City, FL. Upon graduating from Pinecrest High School in December 1953, he enlisted in the USAF January 1954. After basic training at Lackland AFB he was assigned to Lowry AFB to attend the Camera Repair, later known as "Sensors" Tech. School.

Spent his entire career of 26 years in this field of aerial reconnaissance until retiring in 1980. His Phantom (RF-4C) association was field training at Shaw AFB 1965-66, Kadena AB 1966-67 and Mt. Home AFB 1968-69. His last tour of the RF-4C was field shop in the 460th TRW, Tan Son Nhut AB in 1970. He salutes all of the brave men that died and the ones that survived flying the "recce" missions in the RF-4C and RF-101C, it took courage to perform their missions against the odds.

JOEL THOMAS "TOM" CONEY, Major, born Dec. 22, 1942 in Miami, FL. Joined the service in 1965 and trained at Shaw AFB, SC in 1967; Davis-Monthan AFB, AZ in 1968; MacDill AFB, FL in 1977 and Luke AFB, AZ in 1978.

Served with the 360th TRW/16th TRS; 36th TFW/53rd TFS; HQ TAC, 8th TFW/35th TFS; 56th TFW/63rd TFS and 13th TFS; HQ USAFTAWC.

Memorable Experiences: 100 Missions over North Vietnam, he was in last F-4 out of Wheelus AB, Libya; participated in four NATO Tiger Meets; returning to flying after a HQ Tour, Kunsan AFB, Korea; representing and addressing industry at the Reno RF-4 retirement.

He received the Distinguished Flying Cross, 17 Air Medals, Meritorious Service Medal and etc.

Currently he is vice president for Recon/Optical, Inc. at the Washington, DC office. Married, he has three sons.

Other Significant Achievements: Being Alive!

CLARK D. CREBER, born in Toronto, Ontario, Canada and moved to the States when only 5 years old. While in college decided to take a semester off during the Vietnam conflict, bad mistake. Enlisted in the Air Force in 1966. After Lackland AFB, was sent to Sheppard AFB for technical training as mechanic. First assignment was to Reese AFB with Air Training Command. Trained a great deal of pilots for the Air Force. Reese during that time was busier than Chicago's O'Hare with number of take-offs and landings. In 1968 went to RAF Bentwaters and was crew chief on F-4C tail number 64-0887, which was later sold to Spain where it still exists.

Most memorable event other than seeing Europe at Uncle Sam's expense was the shooting down of a C-130 that a crew chief had stolen from another RAF base in England. TDY was at Wheelus AFB, their great bombing range.

After the Air Force, college was completed at Texas Wesleyan University with a BBA. He is now a computer consultant working out of the home, with expertise in AutoCAD. Divorced with no children, he enjoys the Phantom Conventions and tries to make as many as possible.

JOSEPH P. "DOC" DOUGHERTY, born Oct. 5, 1949 in Philadelphia, PA. Entered the service January 1969 and attended basic at Lackland AFB, TX and WCS technical training at Lowry AFB, FL.

Served with 4533rd TTS (T), Eglin AFB, FL in 1969-70; 8th AMS, 8th TFW,

UBON RTAFB in 1970-72 and 58th AMS, Luke AFB, AZ in 1972-73.

Discharged as sergeant G-4 in January 1973.

His memorable experience was working on Paughway I and II TV and laser bombs.

Currently he is an operating engineer.

DAVID B. "FRITO" GARCIA, born Jan. 19, 1945 in Modesto, CA. Entered the service November 1967. Trained AOCS January 1968, NFO VT-10 April 1968, RIO October 1968 and VF-121 February 1969.

Served with VF-121, VF-92, NAF China Lake, USS *Midway*; VF-302, NAS Bermuda, PMTC PT MU6U.

His memorable experience was with VF-92 and CVW-9 aboard USS *Constellation* May 10, 1972, when air wing bagged eight MiGs. He flew 400 combat missions in SEA, 500 traps aboard seven different carriers and 2,000 plus hours in a F-4.

Discharged May 1988 as 04, he received the DFC, two individual Air Medals and 17 Strike/Flight Air Medals.

Currently single, he is a senior data analyst with Summit Research Corp. for COMSEVENTHFLT, NB Yokoshuka, Japan, where he resides.

STEPHEN P. GRZESZCZAK, born Dec. 9, 1941 in Bayonne, NJ. Entered the service in 1958 and trained at Fort Bragg, NC 1958-60 and Okinawa 1960-62. Served with 82nd ABN Div., 2nd ABN Battlegroup, 503rd Inf., Co. E.

His memorable experience was getting his private pilot license. Discharged in 1962 as E-4, he received the Paratrooper Badge.

Currently he is in cargo sales with Continental Airline, Newark, NJ.

Married to Mary, he has two sons, LCD Steve Jr., Navy Seals and Lt. Eric, pilot, USMCR C-130.

LEE HALE, Capt., USMC, got the flying bug from his brother, Rich, a USAF F-100 pilot. After the completion of pilot training in October 1968, Lee was assigned to VMCJ-3, a composite reconnaissance squadron at MCAS El Toro, CA. There he flew the EF-10B, formerly known as the F-3D Skyknight and the RF-4B, in the squadron's roles of electronic and photo reconnaissance.

During his two years at El Toro, the EF-1OBs were retired and Lee was involved in ferrying one to the Marine Corps Air Museum at Quantico, VA for permanent display. Eventually he transferred to MCAS Iwakuni, Japan, where he finished his tour of duty in the Marine Corps flying the RF-4B exclusively. As the squadron "log hog," he managed to accumulate approximately 700 hours in the Phabulous Phantom by flying lots of miserable late night maintenance hops and weekend cross countries. A career highlight involved playing war games with a Navy carrier group sailing through the straits of Japan. After completing a recon run on the carrier, he was vectored toward a bogey that turned out to be a Soviet cruiser that had been shadowing the carrier group for days. Presumably the Soviet sailors enjoyed the air show and smiled for the numerous shots taken with the recon Phantom's on-board systems.

After Marine Corps service, Lee continued his career in corporate (business) aviation logging almost 5,000 hours in the Cessna Citation as a sales demonstration pilot, corporate pilot and flight department manager and chief pilot. He later joined the airlines to fly for Air California and American in the B-737, MD-80, B-757, B-767 and B-777. He still considers the Phantom his best flying experience ever.

MICHAEL R. "F-4", "MIKE GLAZE" HALL, born Jan. 13, 1966 in Fort Riley, KS. Entered the service April 1989. Attended USAF basic training at Lackland AFB, TX, April-May 1989; Tactical Aircraft Maintenance School, Sheppard AFB, TX, May-August 1989; F-4 FTD School, Bergstrom AFB, TX, August-September 1989 and F-4 AMQP School, Spangdahlem, Germany, November-December 1989.

Served with 52nd TFW, 23rd FS, Spangdahlem AFB, Germany, F-4G; 12th OMS, Randolph AFB, TX, T-38A and 169th FG, McEntire, ANGB, SC, F-16A/B, F-16 C/D.

His memorable experiences: Easy question, his most memorable experience in the USAF and in his life had to be his F-4 incentive flight. His flight took place at Spangdahlem AFB, Germany while he was assigned to the 52nd TFW, 23rd FG. His flight was in F-4 0244 and they were part of a four ship (2 F-4s and 2 F-16s) on an air to air mission. After takeoff and the "after burner surge" they split into two separate groups to begin their training mission. His pilot was Capt. Baxley. WOW! What a ride, he was of course flying as the "back seater" but could offer nothing more than my set of eyes to help pick up the "enemy jets and pass it on to his pilot. He did pick up the attack from 2:00 high but was unable to alert Capt. Baxley before he also spotted them. He slammed on the speed brakes and rolled them over on their back and picked up the F-16s tail as he overshot their plane. They did air to air for about 30 minutes and then did their thing. His pilot let him fly the plane for about 30 minutes, which was a wonderful experience. He is a radio controlled model airplane pilot and one flies the stick the same way as in a real aircraft. He put a few moves on the plane that prompted his pilot to say, "give me a little warning before you do some of that RC stuff!" In a flash (actually 1-1/2 hours) the flight was over as they rolled in on Spangdahlem and did five passes over the field before "Bingo" fuel landed them.

What a wonderful time. One that he will remember and cherish for the rest of his life. He will also remember what his pilot said to him as they ended the flight, "Can you actually believe I get paid to do this?" He was so excited he even went back to work and didn't realize that he was on a day off status because of the incentive flight. His buddies reminded him of that after he had put in another 12 hour shift!

During Desert Storm, his aircraft 0274, became a CANN jet because it was the first to break with a shortage of parts. When the parts were available, Sgt. Ron Davis and he returned the aircraft to FMC status in two 12 hour shifts. The 0274 then flew its next five combat sorties, Code 1s.

In March during Desert Storm, his jet maintained a 98.3 percent mission capable rate, 20.3 percent above the USAFE Standard. Also, his jet (0274) flew 41 combat sorties with a total of 111 hours and an 80.2 percent FMC.

He was promoted from below the zone to SRA in February 1991 and in June 1991 he received an Incentive F-4 Flight in F-4G 69-0244.

Awarded AFCM, AFAM, JM Unit Award, AF Outstanding Unit Award w/V, AFGCM, ARF Meritorious Service Medal, NDSM, Southwest Asia Service Medal, AF Overseas Lon Tour Ribbon, AF Longevity Service Award Ribbon, AF Training Ribbon and Small Arms Expert Marksmanship Ribbon.

Currently he is an associate with BMW Manufacturing Corporation. An US Army "Brat," he is from a long line of military family with military ties from the 1750s, father an Army brigadier general, brother an Army major and two uncles with the USAF and Navy. Married with a son and daughter.

MICHAEL TIMOTHY "MIKE" HALL, born in 1941 and raised in Ocean Beach (San Diego), CA. After stints at UCLA and the Naval Academy, Mike was commissioned a 2nd lieutenant, USMCR and received his wings through the MARCAD program in March 1965. At MCAS El Toro, Mike flew F-8s with VMF(AW)-122 until transitioning to F-4Bs in early 1966.

In July 1966, he joined VMFA-542 in Chu Lai, RVN. In February 1967, Mike was assigned to the 1st Marine Div. as a forward air controller. By then a captain, he returned to CONUS in July 1967 with over 100 missions flown. Mike was awarded the DFC and Air Medal for heroism, the Purple Heart, five Strike/Flight Air Medals and the RVN Cross of Gallantry w/Palm.

Mike is a commercial real estate developer. He received a MBA, 1972 and PhD, 1978 from USC. Has three children: Kimberly, Kirsten and Brian and seven grandchildren. He still flies a variety of civilian aircraft.

ROLAND D. HAMBLIN became aware of the F-4 during the early 1970s while at school, and became "hooked" a few years later at the RNAS Museum in Cornwall when he spotted several RN Phantoms sported Jubilee markings (1977, the Queen's Jubilee year). A visit to RAF Greenham Common to IAT 1979 brought an encounter with the specially painted Alcock and Brown RAF F-4M, along with his first F-4. Regular visits to the annual Mildenhall airshow from 1981 to 1991 and the IAT during the 1980s brought Turkish, Spanish and German; RNAS Yeovilton in June 1994 brought Greek, and RAF Lakenheath during the mid 1990s brought Egyptian F-4s into his log book.

He has since logged hundreds of F-4s in Tucson, Pima, Mojave, and AMARC, among others, and still plans to visit Greece, Turkey, Spain and Germany to log as many more as possible.

FRANK HAMBY, born June 25, 1955 in Birmingham, AL. Since he does not have a military background, he offers a layman's early impression of the F-4 Phantom II.

In 1963 his uncle was an avid plastic model aircraft builder.

One such model that he built was the old Aurora F-4 kit, he believes it was marked as the F-110.

In September 1965 National Geographic ran a large article on the USAF and he will always be impressed by the picture. The ordinance variety that the F-4C could carry was very impressionable on a 10-year old.

While on a family vacation in Panama City, FL in June 1968, he saw a F-4 in flight for the first time. After reading sporadically over the last couple of years about the F-4 (from the above article mostly) he finally saw what the fuss was about. He thought "it's so ugly, how does it fly!"

He works for the design/build department for the University of Alabama in Birmingham and has had one of his articles published by their journal in 1996.

RICHARD C. "RICK" HARTNACK, Capt., USMCR, born Nov. 17, 1945 in Los Angeles is a California native and graduate of UCLA with an MBA from Stanford University. Commissioned a 2nd lieutenant through the Platoon Leaders Class Program in June 1967. He attended the Basic School at Quantico and was then assigned to NAS Pensacola where he received his Naval Flight Officer's Wings in late 1968.

After RIO training at NAS Glynco and transition training in the F4-B at MCAS Cherry Point, he was assigned to the VMFA-451 "Warlords" at MCAS Beaufort. In August 1969 he joined the VMFA-115 "Silver Eagles" in Chu Lai, RVN. During his year in combat he flew 220 missions and won the Navy Commendation Medal w/Combat V and 14 Air Medals. In August 1970 he reported to MCAS, Yuma and the newly formed VMFAT-101 "Sharpshooters" where he served as an instructor and adjutant.

He left the Marines in September 1971 to pursue a career in banking. He serves today as the vice chairman of Union Bank of California, the 25th largest bank in the country and lives in Los Angeles. Married to Dail for 32 years, he has three children: Kathleen, Eric and Brian. He is an active pilot and flies his own plane on business frequently.

CARL HELLIS, born July 20, 1945 in Marysville, CA. Entered the service in 1967 and trained at Mather AFB, CA and Homestead AFB, FL. Served with 436 TFS (FUE) Homestead AFB, S23 TFS/405 FW, Clark AB, PI (F-4D); 10 TFS/50 TFW, Hahn AB, Germany, (F-4D) and 123 FS/142 FW, Oregon, (F101B/F/F4-C).

Memorable experience: the Mosel River Valley with Hahn friends, William Tell 1984-1986-1988.

Retired from the USAF as lieutenant colonel in 1995 and received 20 years worth of Air Force awards.

Currently he is self-employed with a small business and Mr. Mom to a 4-year old. Married to Lori A., an attorney, he has a daughter Kjersten A.

MIKE "B.D." HOLLOWAY, born in the Heart of Dixie, Birmingham, AL and raised just off the end of the runway at the Birmingham Airport. Mike grew up watching the RF-84Fs of the Alabama Air National Guard's 117th Tact. Recon. Wing take off and land within 150 yards of his front door. Mike's uncle, a full-member of the guard and crew chief of one of the unit's RF-84s, would take Mike with him to the base and introduced him to the aircraft and camaraderie of the unit personnel. When the local Air Guard switched to RF-4Cs in 1971, Mike watched the first Phantoms arrive.

The first thing he did upon graduating high school in May 1973 was to join the Air Guard as a security policeman. Mike began working at the Air Guard full time after returning from basic training and Technical School. He began photographing the unit's RF-4 aircraft to pass the long hours he spent alone on the flight line and as a way to learn photography. It did not take long, however, for this past time to become a full time passion for documenting these aircraft.

As the end of the 117th RW Phantom era approached, Mike, along with other volunteers, gave of his off duty time to assist in the application of special markings to select unit aircraft for posterity. On May 26, 1994 he was on duty when the last operational Birmingham RF-4Cs departed, marking the end of 23 years of Phantom flights through the skies of Alabama.

SMSgt. Holloway is currently the security forces squadron superintendent for the 117th Air Refueling Wing in Birmingham, AL and has served with the 117th for 26 years.

THOMAS R. HUGHES, born Feb. 19, 1947 in Barnesville, OH. Entered the service July 1966 and attended basic training at Lackland AFB, Tech School at Amarillo AFB, September 1966 and AFSC J43151C. Served with the 49th TFW Holloman AFB, NM and 8TFS, 22TFS, 36th Bitburg AFB, Germany.

Memorable experiences: a ride in the back seat of F-4; seeing Athens, Greece; Paris, France; Venice, Italy and Tripoli, Libya. He was promoted to E-5 in three years; crew chief for wing commander of 49th TFW. Their phase dock crew received first zero defect inspection in USAFE at 22 TFS, Bitburg AFB.

Discharged July 1970 as staff sergeant (E-5), he was awarded Good Conduct Medal, National Defense Medal, Presidential Unit Citation and Air Force Outstanding Unit Award.

Currently he is an aviation maintenance technician with 33 years experience.

Married to Debbie, he has two children, Matthew and Melissa.

JAN "JAKE" JACOBS, Cmdr., hails from Arkansas, the state that produced Navy legend Jimmy Thatch long before anybody heard of Bill Clinton. While attending Arkansas Polytechnic College, he was accepted into the Aviation Reserve Officer Candidate (AVROC) program and finished the first half of AOCS at Pensacola between his junior and senior years. He returned to Pensacola after graduation and was commissioned in November 1971. While in training, he was selected as a Distinguished Naval Graduate and received a regular commission.

After designation as a Naval flight officer in June 1972, Jan reported to VF-121 as a replacement F-4 RIO and then joined VF-21 in March 1973. After a tour with the Freelancers on board *Ranger* (CVA-61) and subsequent overseas shore duty, he resigned from the Navy in 1977 and accepted a Reserve commission. Based at Miramar, he served as RIO in the F-4 and F-14 before retiring from the Naval Reserve in 1992.

In 1978, Jan volunteered for the Tailhook Association, serving *The Hook* staff as editor of the Navy Reserve column, "Manning the Spare." He also worked part-time as the "At Marshal" editor in the early 1980s. Nearing completion of his Reserve duty, Jan succeeded Barrett Tillman as managing editor of *The Hook* in 1989. As such, he provided continuity between the tenures of editors Bob Lawson and Steve Milikin in 1990-91.

Jan's extensive computer knowledge has been a major factor in permitting in-house production of the magazine. He also publishes *Smoke Trails*, the Journal of the F-4 Phantom II Society.

DON "DJ" JAY, a North Carolinian AKA "Flying Tar Heel" whose first Phantom phright was at Eglin in 1966. A phriendly Air Force captain persuaded him to sign up for a 20 plus year hitch. Three sea tours, 13 PCSs, seven countries later he is back where he started in North Carolina.

Over 50K slides reside in one room of the house. Lots of little yellow boxes multiply in this room. He is concentrating on the Fox Four Echo but can't pass up a good slide. Photography has made many friends and few enemies, but on the whole a great way to meet folks who enjoy the same pastime.

He is a member of AAHS, AFA, Tailhook, Phantom Society and AARP.

WAYNE JOHNSON, joined the Marines in 1970 and after training reported to VMFA-314 as a radar technician on F-4Bs. He crewed for 314s first F-4N at Top Gun Class 06-73.

Transferred to Japan in 1974, Wayne was assigned to MAG-15 Avionics and was promoted to staff sergeant.

Returning stateside in 1975, Wayne rejoined VMFA-314 and by 1978 was the acting NCOIC of the squadron QA Division.

Leaving the Marines, he joined Douglas Aircraft and was involved in FAA certification efforts for the MD-80 and KC-10 aircraft and the launch of the T-45 and C-17 programs. He was supervisor of the Douglas QA Procedures department for nearly 10 years.

Wayne joined the C-17 division in 1995 to prepare FAA-compliant quality systems for the proposed MD-17. He prepared the McDonnell Douglas and then the Boeing, corporate-level ISO 9001 quality manuals and has worked with national and international teams on aerospace quality standard development.

RICHARD KIERBOW, entered the Air Force in 1964. Attended undergraduate pilot training at Webb AFB, TX, 1964-65. He flew T-37B, T-38A, KC-135A and 02A.

Discharged in 1984 as major, he was awarded the DFC, Air Medal w/9 OLCs and two Presidential Unit Citations.

He received a bachelor of industrial engineering from Georgia Tech and a master of science in engineering administration from St. Mary's University, TX. He is retired.

DAVID RICHARD "NEETS" KUNTZ, born Feb. 7, 1951 in Philadelphia, PA. Entered the service July 1968 and trained at Lowry AFB, CO.

Served with 366th TFW, Da Nang AFB, May 1969-70; 4453 CCTW, Davis-Monthan AFB, AZ, May 1970-71; 58TFTW June 1971, Luke AFB, AZ; 432nd UDORN RTAB January-May 1972.

Memorable experiences: Hot tuning AIM-7 Sparrow missiles for several MiG killers, including Capt. Steve Ritchie during Linebacker II; watching "Max Effort" bombing mission take-off at Da Nang. He flew in a F-106B 59-0149 on a five hour mission to Davis Monthan AFB, to close out 16 Air Defense Alert Mission with F-106s. Launching ATR-2A "Genie" and AIM-7G "Falcon" during combat pike deployment to Tyndall AFB, FL and hitting the Drone.

Discharged July 1972 as E-4 and joined the Air National Guard in November 1973. Presently he is an E-6. Awarded AFAM, Joint Meritorious Unit Award, AF OUA, Vietnam Service Medal w/4 Devices, Air Force Overseas Long-Tour Ribbon, RVN Gallantry Cross w/Device and RVN Campaign Medal.

Married to Jerrianne, he has a son, Peter.

RALPH G. LANGLEY JR., born April 9, 1946 in Glendale, CA. Entered the service Dec. 7, 1965 and attended basic training at Lackland AFB, TX. Other training places: Kingsley Field, OR, 1966 (F-101B, F); Takhli, Thailand, 1968 (F-105 D, F, EB-66); Torrejon AB, Spain, 1969 (F-100, F-4 C,D,E); Nellis AFB, NV 1972 (FB-111A); Nevada Air National Guard 1973 (RF-101B); Nevada Air National Guard 1975 (RF-4C) and Nevada Air National Guard 1995 (C-103E).

Served with 408th CAMS, Kingsley Field, OR; 355th FMS, Takhli, Thailand; 613th TFS and 401 OMS, Torrejon AB, Spain; 434th TFS, Nellis AFB and 152 TRS, Reno, NV.

His memorable experiences include being the first crew chief of F-4E 68-391 when it came out of the factory in Torrejon, Spain in 1970 and winning RAM 1990 before going to Desert Shield/Storm.

Awarded Meritorious Service Medal, AFCM w/OLC, AFAM w/5 OLCs, PUC, AF OUA w/7 OLCs, Vietnam Service Medal, Southwest Asia Service Medal, RVN Gallantry Cross w/Palm, RVN Campaign Medal, Kuwait Liberation Medal, plus numerous other awards and decorations.

Currently he serves as a senior master sergeant, air technician with the Nevada Air National Guard and has 34 years of service. Married, he has two children.

ANDY LEE, is 25 years of age and working as an airframe technician in a local aerospace company on the F-5.

He first got interested in the Phantom when his Dad first bought him a 1/48 kit of Ritchie's F-40 (66-7463). His first thought was "Gee, this is one ugly bird." but after reading up on the Vietnam War, that changed to respect and awe. It seems the F-4s were everywhere. Killing MiGs, dropping bombs and annihilating SAMS.

By chance he got Paul Collins' address from a magazine and decided to join up. It has been about 10 years now and he has yet to regret it. The first Phantom he ever saw was during Phancon 1993 in Birmingham. He remembers his heartbeat getting faster as the plane taxied into the gate and he looked out the window and saw all those RF-4Cs parked on the other side. He has since attended Phancon 1994 and 1999. Also, he visited Rhein-Hapsten, Germany in 1995. These were probably the best moments in his life. There's nothing in the world like a couple of F-4s taking off in full burners. The sight and the roar of these J-79s! "You'd have to be there to understand."

To get over Phantom withdrawal syndrome, he also built models in his spare time. Also looking at his photos and books help some. As he writes this he is already looking forward to the next Phancon where he can again be among a great bunch of guys and a "phantastic" airplane.

Finally, in case any lawn part lovers out there read this and wonder what the fuss is about and their's is a better plane that can do everything better. Well, get this, before multi-role became the in-thing, the Phantom was already doing it. She has killed more SAMS, dropped more bombs and created more MiG parts than any other planes out there. The Phantom has seen it all and done it all.

DON LEGGER, MSgt., in spring 1969, he was a member of the USAF stationed at Camranh Bay, VN. He remembers it to be a sunny day with some scattered clouds. He was a technician in the avionic shop (Automatic Flight Control Systems), Maintenance Squadron. At that time they had over 120 F-4 Phantoms, Cs and Ds mostly.

New recruits came in all forms even backseat wizzos, yes! He was in his first week in-country, a 1st lieutenant on the runway flying with a very experienced pilot. The pilots were in their final check out, the engines were running and continuing down the list the auto pilot switch would not engage. The aircraft would not get clearance for take-off without this function.

That day was his day in the rotation for red ball duty. Red ball is a term that describes a last minute adjustment or repair before take-off. If this repair or adjustment fails the aircraft's mission will be aborted and some troops in the bush will not get their air support. The automatic flight control amplifier is located in the port side, backseat, behind a thin metal panel.

Well, he got the call and jumped out of the line truck. With tuning tool he ran to the aircraft with engines running, approached the left wing, climbed on the wing tank to the wing and to the fuselage. The backseat man looked up and he motioned for him to sit back, he looked at the hammer with widest eyes and "what are you going to do with that?" At that time he hit the side of the kick panel effectively hitting the front of the amplifier and jarring loose the stuck relay. The backseat man retried the automatic flight control switch and it stayed engaged, the function was working again. The lieutenant looked at him with surprise and amazement, he will never forget the look on his face.

ROBERT HAMPTON "BOB" LEGRAND JR., born Feb. 19, 1943 in Philadelphia, PA. Entered the service in 1970. Trained as a flight surgeon at Brooks AFB, San Antonio, TX. Served with 480 TFS, Vietnam, Phu Cat and 91 TRS, Bergstrom AFB.

Memorable experiences include fighter missions over Vietnam, Laos and Cambodia.

Discharged as major in 1972, he was awarded the Bronze Star, DFC w/OLC and Air Medal w/2 OLCs.

Currently he is a neurosurgeon and is married to Jean Ann with six children.

DEAN A. MARCUCCI, born and raised in California and son of a Navy plane captain. Dean's father Al has owned an aircraft business since the 1960s and Dean has benefited from exposure to aviation ever since. While in high school and during his undergraduate years in college, Dean contributed to the family business by overhauling general aviation and WWII-vintage military aircraft ignition systems, to include the majority of participants in the annual Reno National Championship Air Races.

Following college, Dean was unsuccessful in pursuing a military flying career as neither the USAF or USN at the time were accepting applicants. Since 1990, Dean has worked for the Federal government in various capacities with the EPA, Department of the Interior and the Department of Defense. He returned to graduate school and received a MS in 1995. Since that time, Dean has served as a special agent for the USAF, Office of Special Investigations and has conducted criminal and counterintelligence investigations in support of USAF people, materials and operations. He is currently assigned to Secretary of the Air Force for Acquisition and supports new technologies and weapon systems.

Dean first became interested in the F-4 Phantom during the mid-1970s. Living close to NAS Alameda, CA he had many opportunities to see and hear the F-4 in its prime. He began collecting books, photos and patches pertinent to the Phantom and has never stopped. He has been a member of the society for over 10 years. Dean has been a past contributor to *Smoke Trails* and has also observed the Phantom in its golden years by attending several society conventions and other events. Despite his exposure to types preceding and succeeding the F-4, the Phantom will "Phorever" be Dean's favorite airplane.

PATRICK MARTIN, grew up on both sides of the "pond," Europe and Canada while bouncing around different Canadian Armed Forces bases. After graduating from Kwantlen College in business administration he worked in the accounting field.

The aviation hobby turned serious after retirement. He writes for several journals and has published four aviation books to date: *Tail Code*, the complete history of USAF tactical aircraft tail code marking 1966-1990; *Hook Code*, USN & USMC the complete history of USN & USMC tail code markings 1963-1994; *The Index*: An aviation resource index cross reference guide and Canadian Armed Forces aircraft finish and markings 1968-1997.

In the pursuit of writing, he has flown with many units in Canadian and US forces. These included several carrier traps.

Patrick resides in British Columbia and is married with five children. He continues writing in the aviation field with the Phantom as a staple for chosen reading material.

JEFF MASON, a 52 year old electrical engineer and who lives with his very understanding wife in North East England.

His interest in the F-4 started in the 1960s and stemmed mainly from building plastic aircraft kits.

At the time the Phantom entered service it was quite a radical shape and for him the twin nosewheels, separated in-line cockpits, cranked wing and tail surfaces and overall bulk made it stand out from the fighters which were then in service.

The fact that the more stores that were hung underneath made it look even better and its introduction into service with the RAF and Royal Navy increased its charisma.

From then on he couldn't get enough of anything even remotely connected with the aircraft and he eagerly sought every kit, book and magazine article connected with it, particularly the superb Japanese publications.

At airshows the F-4s were always looked at the longest and the crews questioned about any changes or additions to their aircraft. Some lasting memories of the Phantom are seeing a new in-service RAF F-4 seemingly being flown around a tree in the Yorkshire Dales, the USAF RF-4C crew at the 25th anniversary met at Greenham Common who had proudly bought and applied the large circular anniversary logo to the intake of their aircraft only to be told by their wingmen that "It looks OK, now but don't bank on the CO being happy when he sees it!" and the RAF 56 squadron crewman who told him that the target identification periscope fitted in the rear cockpit of his now elderly aircraft had "probably been taken from an old Army tank."

The ultimate privilege however was seeing a tight 16 ship box formation being flown at an airshow at Conningsby Lincolnshire. The Wattisham based aircraft had flown over London to salute the

Queen's birthday and had returned via Conningsby where they flew two circuits of the airfield.

Toward the end of the second circuit, the aircraft on the inside of the turn seemed to be getting ever close to the ground and as they leveled off and headed for home the formation noticeably "eased."

A couple of F-4 regrets are that, having collected lots of Phantom data, he was rash enough on separate occasions to criticize details on a couple of fairly well known paintings of the aircraft only to be told both times that F-4 pilots had given them their approval. (Two of those occasions when he was sure that he was right but wish he had kept his mouth shut anyway).

Over the past 30 plus years he has amassed a large collection of books and articles and an even larger collection of unbuilt plastic kits, (many sent by his pen pal Joe Joinville in Ohio). He still gets a big kick out of the release of anything new on the "Phabulous Phantom."

ROBERT "BOB" MATTSON, born and brought up in Massachusetts, went to Tri-State University in Indiana for a BS degree in electronics engineering and on to McDonnell Aircraft Corp. in January 1955, retired in January 1991 and moved back "home" to Massachusetts.

Worked as electronic engineer on Talos and GAM-72 Missiles, projects Mercury and Gemini Spacecraft and then to the RF-4C in December 1962. Began F/RF-4 Avionics career as associate engineer responsible for design, installation and integration of the ARC-105 HF Radio Set into the RF-4C. Spent next 29 years working on the F/RF-4 Program, slowly rising through the ranks with increasing responsibility to retire as assistant F-4 program manager and chief F-4 avionics engineer.

Over time, the challenge changed from designing and building newer and better F-4 versions to support of and upgrades to those F/RF-4s in the field.

Life was never boring because when you answered to every avionics system in every model of F/RF-4 aircraft you never knew what the next phone call would bring. Some were dillies.

LONNY K. "EAGLE" MCCLUNG, Capt., USN, RET, born June 30, 1939 in Pana, IL. Graduate of University of Illinois, BSME, NROTC, 1962. Winged 1964. Initial tour VAW-11 LSO, deployed Vietnam (E-2, Constellation). Exchange duty Edwards AFB included USAF Test Pilot School plus two years as classified project officer. Two Vietnam deployments with VF-92 (F-4, Constellation).

MS in administrative science, USNPG School, Monterey. Four aviation commands: VF-51 (F-4, *F.D. Roosevelt*, then F-14 transition); "TOPGUN" (F-5 and A-4); VF-124 (F-14 Fleet Readiness Squadron) NAS Miramar and Training Air Wing 2, NAS Kingsville, TX.

Sea tours: ACOS Operations, Carrier Group 7 (*Ranger*); chief of staff, Cruiser Destroyer Group 3 (*Enterprise*) and chief of staff Second Fleet.

Washington tours: BUPERS PCS program manager; director, Strike/Amphibious Warfare (OP-74). Retired in 1992. Over 1,000 carrier landings, 200 plus Vietnam missions. Awarded DSSM, LOM (3), MSM (2), Air Medal (22), NCM (2) and NAM.

Currently, he is director of Aircraft Development, United Capital Corporation of Illinois. Converting Grumman GIII Albatross Seaplanes to turbo-props.

He was president of the Tailhook Association 1995-99. Married to Audrey for over 34 years, he has a daughter, Kim and son Kurt.

CHARLES R. "CMAC" MCCORMACK, LTC, graduated from the USAF Academy June 7, 1972. After navigator training at Mather and F-4C WSO training with 426th TFTS "Snoopy" at Luke, he reported in August 1974 to the 23rd TFS "Fighting Hawks" at Spangdahlem, W. Germany flying F-4Ds. At Spangdahlem, CMAC was qualified as Pave LORAN, Pave Spike, Maverick and Simulator Instructor. In October 1978 began a 13-month tour at Kunsan AB, ROK as IWSO and FCF WSO with 35th TFS "Panthers". In November 1979 he joined 430th TFS "Tigers" at Nellis and led deployments to Greece and Panama ending his tour as the Wing Stan/Eval WSO. CMAC separated Sept. 28, 1981 after a last F-4 FCF flight on Sept. 25, 1981 with over 1,400 hours in the F-4C/D.

In October 1981 Charlie was hired by Northrop Aircraft and in April 1982 was selected for the classified B-2 program; later working YF-23 fighter and other projects. In June 1991 he left Northrop for Rockwell, now Boeing, to work on aircraft and space programs as a crew systems engineer.

In September 1982, CMAC joined the California ANG with 196th TFS "Grizzlys" at March AFB and over the next 10 plus years was mission ready in the F-4C, F-4E and RF-4C. His F-4 flying ended with a RF-4C boneyard delivery June 17, 1993 and he retired from the ANG, Nov. 7, 1995, with a total of 2,447 hours in F-4C, D, E and RF-4C.

DANIEL H. "DANO" MICHEL, born Nov. 23, 1947 in Huntington, Long Island, NY.

His memorable experience was flight of 16 RF4-C from 117th Reconnaissance Wing doing a flyover at Birmingham MAP, AL at their farewell airshow.

He was a member of the board of directors Jackson (MS) Jaycees in 1982-84 and Jaycee of the Month May 1983. Currently he is the second shift manager in retail sales.

His father (deceased) was a WWII veteran, combat engineer and received two purple hearts and a Bronze Star. He has one sister and his mother is still living.

GREG MILLER, although he did not serve in the armed forces, his encounters with the F-4 were very up close and personal. It was during the spring of 1983 that he moved to an apartment complex in Marietta, GA. Fortunately, it was located directly in the flight path of Dobbins ARB/ Atlanta NAS and the Lockheed Georgia Co. During the next several years he had the opportunity to watch A-7s, C5-Bs, C-130s, as well as many other military aircraft. However, there was one plane that upon takeoff was admittedly the loudest "window rattler" ever heard and could be identified during landing without even seeing it because it screeched and howled like no other. Yes, the Georgia ANG 116th FW flew the F-4Ds as well. It was like having an airshow on your front steps every Saturday and Sunday. Being so fascinated with this extremely unusually sounding plane, he spent many afternoons overlooking the runway to watch the ANG unit drill. Because the runway is very close to US 41 Highway, it was not uncommon to see traffic come to a standstill when the Phantoms began their takeoff. Eventually in 1986 the 116th replaced the Phantoms with the F-15. However, it just didn't seem as exciting to watch the more perfect, modern planes like the F-15. The Phantom just stood out! In 1996, the Georgia 116th moved to Robbins AFB and converted to a bomber wing.

All is quiet now at the Marietta base, except for an occasional F/A-18 or a C-130 from Atlanta NAS. However, parked outside of the Dobbins ARB entrance on US 41 are several planes from the past. As he drives by, he always looks for that one, the F-4D with Georgia ANG insignia. He remembers the sights and sounds, as well as the great fun that he had and how privileged he was to be able to watch the greatest jet fighter ever built.

JEFFREY L. NICHOLSON, born Oct. 29, 1953 in Washington, DC. His love for aviation began early in life. Growing up outside Washington, DC, he spent many summer days sitting on the flightline at Andrews AFB with his grandfather while his father was at work. The "thunder and aroma" of jet operations had him hooked. The 113th TFW was flying the F-100 at that time and it would be almost 20 years later until they would transition to the Phantom. Now, as an adult, the rumbling of the ground and the rattling of the window panes early in the morning as the engines would run up prior to ground roll is firmly engraved in his memory. What a way to awaken. Most assuredly, something no alarm clock can reproduce.

In his den hangs a print of a pilot in the "office" of an F-4 accompanied by a verse by Ernest Hemmingway, other members may have a copy. It reads: "You love a lot of things if you are around them, but there isn't any woman and there isn't any horse not any before nor any after, that is as lovely as a great airplane. And men who love them are faithful to them even though they leave them for others. Man has one virginity to lose in fighters and if it is a lovely airplane he loses it to, there is where his heart will forever be." Enough said?

Currently he is employed in nuclear medicine technology.

EARL L. "TOOT" OTTO, born Jan. 10, 1928 in Pateros, WA. Entered the service April 1948. Attended basic at Lackland AFB, TX; Jet Mechanic School, Chanute AFB, IL, August 1948-February 1949 and munitions maintenance training, Lowry AFB, CO, July 1965.

Served with 78th FTR Group, 82nd FTR Sqdn., Hamilton AFB; 51st FTR Group, 16th FTR Sqdn., Naha, Okinawa; Itazuke, Japan; Kimpo, Korea; Tsuiki, Japan and Suwon, Korea; 101st Field Maint., 62nd Field Maint., Larson AFB; 1624th Support Sqdn., Earnest Harmon AFB; 325th Field Maint., McChord AFB; 303rd Munitions Maint., Bien Hoa AB, Vietnam and 57th FTR Group, Paine Field, WA.

Retired from the USAF May 1968 as MSgt (E-7). Awarded Army Good Conduct Medal, USAF Good Conduct Medal, Korean Service w/2 OLCs, UN Service, Korean Presidential Unit Citation, Vietnam Service, Vietnam Campaign, USAF Longevity, NDSM and USAF Commendation Medal.

He was not assigned to any F-4 units, but remembers getting chills up and down his spine watching Thunderbirds and Blue Angels F-4s at airshows. All that noise and power! He found out about the F-4 Society from Doug Remington (member deceased in 1987), a real dedicated F-4 nut. The only experience Earl had with a real F-4 was at McChord AFB in 1964. A Marine F-4 had landed and could not start the left engine. After a lot of trouble shooting, they could not find out what was wrong with it, so the Marine Squadron sent a crew with a replacement engine.

Retired from the Washington state service, he was married 31 years, widowed in 1989, no children and hasn't remarried, yet.

GLEN D. "MAGIC" OWEN, LTC, USAF, RET, born Jan. 9, 1949 in Concordia, KS. Entered the service June 1971. Served with 1st TFW, 27th TFS, MacDill AFB, FL, May-December 1973.

Served with 80th TFS, Kunsan AB, South Korea; 32nd TFS, "Wolfhounds," Soesterberg AB, Netherlands; 113th TFS "Racers," Indiana ANG, Terre Haute, IN and 184th TFG "Jayhawks," McConnell AFB, KS.

His memorable experiences include flying 2,047.1 hours in F-4 C, D and E, instructor WSO and EWO. Last flight in F-4 March 30, 1990 F-4D, 65-680 to Davis-Monthan AFB, AZ. First flight May 1973 with Maj. Woods with the seat stuck in full up and locked position. Alert tours in Korea, Germany, Netherlands and the earthquake in Aviana in 1976. Retired September 1994.

Currently employed as an intelligence analyst at National Intelligence Center, Wright-Patterson AFB, OH. Married to Donita, he has three children.

ALEX RODRIGUEZ JR., born in Miami, FL, home to the Miami Dolphins and Florida Marlins. Graduated high school and went directly to the USMC in 1988. In the Corps, he served with the 7th Marine Exped. Bn., May 1989; 4th Air Naval Gunfire Liaison Co., November 1989 and the 4th Marine Recon. Bn. He is cur-

rently in the reserves and holds the rank of staff sergeant.

His memorable moments in the Corps were calling in ordinance from a pair of F-4S from El Toro air station and working with Air Guard F-4s in Puerto Rico. The most thrilling was by far, jumping out of hi-performance aircraft such as OV-10 Broncos and C-141s. He has earned the coveted Gold Naval Jump Wings, a Meritorious Unit Citation, Marine Corps Medal and expert badges in both the M-16A2 and M-9 pistol.

His experience in the Marine Corps has given him the opportunity to further serve his country as a federal agent with the US Border Patrol Marine Enforcement unit in Miami. He has been in the Border Patrol since 1994 and continues to interdict contraband and migrants entering the US illegally.

His first experience with the Phantom, was fishing in the Florida Keys with his dad. He saw two jets make several low passes over us at about 200 feet. He asked his dad what they were and his dad smartly replied "Phantoms."

He currently enjoys adding to his 50 plus Phantom model collection with permission from his lovely wife Jhara and daughter Victoria Alexis.

STEPHEN B. SCHEFFRIN, MSgt., RET, USAFR, born May 21, 1952 in Jamaica, NY, but considers Miami, FL to be his hometown. Enlisted in the Air Force October 1970. Attended basic training at Lackland AFB, TX; Avionics School and Airborne Radar School, Keesler AFB, MS and Senior NCO Academy.

Units served with the USAF, 309th TFS (F-4E), 31 AMS (F-4E) Homestead AFB, FL; 307th TFS (F-4D/E, RF-4C), 432nd AMS, Udorn RTAFB, Thailand; 56th AMS (OV-10, EC-47, HH-53, T-39) Nakhon Phanom RTAFB, Thailand and 456th AMS (KC-135Q, B-52G), Beale AFB, CA. Units with the USAFR, 79th AEWCS (EC-121) Homestead AFB, FL; 445th AMS (C-141A/B), Norton AFB, FL; 68th CAMS, (KC-135, KC-10), Seymour Johnson AFB, NC; 93rd ILMS, (KC-135, B-52H) Castle AFB, CA and HQ ACC, Langley AFB, VA.

His memorable experiences include serving in the 432nd AMS when Capt.'s. Ritchey, DeBellevue and Feinstein became Aces and with the 56th AMS, TDY at Ubon RTAFB when the Vietnam War ended.

Discharged from the USAF October 1974 and retired from USAFR May 1994. Awarded PUC, Armed Forces Reserve Medal, Vietnam Service Medal, Air Reserve Meritorious Service Medal, AF Good Conduct Medal, RVN Campaign Medal, Expeditionary Forces Medal, AF Crew Member Wings and Master Munitions Maintenance Badge.

Received BS from Southern Illinois University in 1980; associate of applied science, Community College of the AF, 1989 and a graduate of the AFSC Quality Assurance Civilian Intern Program. Currently a civilian employee of the USAF, Logistics Management Specialist, GS-12. Formerly NASA Quality Assurance Specialist Space Shuttle, GS-11, Kennedy Space Center, FL. Married to Noothiam in 1976 he has two sons, Daniel and Robert.

PAUL R. "PR" SCHMIDT, LTC, RET, born March 1940 in Appleton, WI. entered the service in 1959. Trained at Shaw AFB in 1971.

Served with 14th Tac Recon Sqdn, Udorn, Thailand and 18th Tac Recon Sqdn, Shaw AFB, SC.

His memorable experiences include Vietnam, linebacker and many fine friends, some lost forever. Eight years and 3,800 hours Phantom time, all in the RF4-C.

Retired in 1979 from the service and currently owns an appraisal practice. He married Bonnie in 1981.

GEOFFREY H. SCOTT, (callsign "Buzzard"), born Sept. 2, 1963 in the Bronx, NY. Joined the Navy in 1981 after high school. Attended basic at Great Lakes, IL, VF-171 first tour.

Served with VF-171 Det. Key West, FL, F-4N/S.

He remembers taking the F-4 to sea with VF-171 and Carrier Air Wing 17 onboard the USS *Saratoga* CV-60 in 1983. He had logged 3,400 flight hours in Naval Aircraft and 316 carrier arrested landings in the C-2A transport aircraft.

Awarded Overseas Service Award w/ Bronze Star, Sea Service Award w/Silver Star and Bronze Star, Antarctica Service Medal, four Good Conduct Medals, HSM, ComNavAirPac "Battle E," MUCR w/2 Bronze Stars, Joint Meritorious Unit Commendation, Southwest Asia Service w/2 Bronze Stars, NDSM, ComNavAirPac Safety Award, NUCR w/Bronze Star and Kuwait Liberation Medal.

Currently single, he is a Naval Flight Officer Flight student, ensign, NAS Pensacola, FL.

THOMAS "SENK" SENKELESKI, born July 23, 1946 in Bayonne, NJ. Entered the service 1966. Attended basic training, Lackland AFB, TX; techical training, Sheppard AFB, TX and combat crew training Davis-Monthan AFB, AZ.

Served with 4453rd CCTW, Arizona in 1966; 366th FMS, Da Nang, Vietnam in 1967; 405th FW Tainan AB (TDY) in 1969; 405th Fighter Wing, 523rd TFS, Clark AFB, Philippines in 1968-69.

Memorable experiences: sitting on sandbag bunker near runway in Da Nang watching a crippled B-52 come screaming by attempting an emergency landing, unfortunately he touched down too late overshooting runway into a minefield. Memorable and disturbing. Things he misses about his Air Force days: crew chief on F-4C in Clark AB, sitting under the bird in the shade venting liquid oxygen into his hat making it frozen to keep cool, the guys he worked with and TDY in Tainan Nuke Alert Pad, great duty. He doesn't miss putting on coveralls and crawling into intake for inspections.

Some of his out of service memorable experiences: touring Spain in 1978 stopping in Pamplona to run with the bulls, only to be running from the Spanish Army clearing streets due to riots breaking out. The festival was canceled on the second day. In 1975 rafting the Colorado River through the Grand Canyon, "Grand" indeed.

Discharged in 1969 as sergeant. Awarded the Vietnam Service Medal and Air Force Commendation Medal.

Currently he is retired after 22 years as a police officer and is on the security force of a nuclear plant in New Jersey. Married to Phyllis for 22 years, he has two children, Lauren and Daniel.

MICHAEL E. "SNUFFY" SMITH,

born April 1, 1952 in Corvallis, OR. He has been pretty lucky and fortunate throughout his life. He grew up on a small farm in the central Willamette Valley in Oregon. Attended Lane Community College where he majored in aviation technology, i.e. learning to fly! He finished his college education at Louisiana Tech University, graduating May 1974 with an USAF ROTC scholarship and a pilot slot. This in itself was amazing, as at this time most pilot candidates were not getting UPT slots, only rated supplements. He went to UPT at Columbus AFB and finished near the top of his class with the Flying Training Award/Trophy.

He was lucky enough to go to RTU at Luke AFB in F-4Cs. He was then assigned to Moody AFB in Valdosta, GA as one of the initial cadre in the 339th TFS, flying F-4Es. After 18 months there he had a remote tour to Korea, where he was again an initial cadre, this time of the 497th TFS "Night Owls" from the 8th TFW Wolfpack, assigned to Taegu AB, flying F-4Ds. Taegu was a ROKAF F-4 base with four ROKAF Squadrons and them with their 12 UE Squadron. After a year there he went to Clark AB, Philippines and spent the next three years flying F-4Es in the 3-TFs. After his Phillippine tour he was assigned a "Weasel" slot and proceeded to George AFB for training, six months in the 561st TFS, the back to the 562nd TFS for 1-1/2 years to teach new Weasels. Again, back to Clark AB for a tour in the infamous 90th TFS "Pair-O-Dice" Sqdn. flying F-4Gs. Here he met his beautiful wife, Faith and from that moment on he has been one of the luckiest fighter pilots ever. From there he went to Eglin AFB where he was assigned to the Tactical Air Warfare Center, TAWC. This was the best assignment he had, testing all kinds of munitions, radars and electronics. He was qualified in all models of the F-4 and regularly flew them all, including the RF-4. He was so lucky to have spent 15 years in the USAF, flew for 15 years and flew the F-4 operationally for 14 of them. He was qualified in every mission the F-4 had and couldn't have asked for a better life.

WAYNE SMITH,

Arizona born and from an Air Force family, joined the Air Force May 1978 and completed six weeks basic military training at Lackland AFB, TX, June 1978. Transferred to the 3373rd Technical Training School at Chanute AFB, IL. There he completed the aircrew Egress Systems course of 228 hours on Aug. 30, 1978.

Arrived duty station George AFB, CA Sept. 7, 1978 and was assigned to the 35th TFW, 35th Equip. Maint. Sqdn. Egress shop. This base was home to the 20th and 21st TFTS F-4E German wing and the 562nd TFTS, 561st and 563rd TFS F-4G Wild Weasels. The base had two tailcodes, "6A" And "WW." He served with this unit from Sept. 23, 1978 until discharged from active duty Aug. 30, 1983.

He was the first senior airman to be certified to clear F-4 Egress final inspections (red x's) which was usually done by a rank of sergeant or above. As flightline dayshift supervisor, he accomplished 95 percent of all red ball conditions.

As Egress Phase chief, he had a 90-93 percent pass rate on inspections during an 18 month period and aided in developing one of the best Egress Sections within the Tactical Air Command. Also, initiated and instructed Egress familiarization classes on safety on and around the ejection seat for maintenance specialists.

As part of his military training at George AFB he completed Aircrew Egress Systems Repairman/Technician course of 90 hours Dec. 22, 1978, the NCO Orientation course March 1981 and USAF Supervisors course August 1982. He received his NCO status as sergeant Jan. 1, 1982 which was his rank on leaving the Air Force.

Participated in many TDYs including Felix Brave 80-2, Bold Eagle 80 and 82 and numerous red flag exercises at Nellis AFB, NV. In his five years of service, a little over one year was TDY deployment.

Awarded AF Training Ribbon, AF Good Conduct Medal, AF Commendation Medal and AF Longevity Service Award Ribbon.

He was selected Egress Person of the Month for October 1981 and received an one hour flight in a F-4G. Persons were selected on recommendation of the shop chief and immediate supervisor along with job performance and APRs.

Currently he is an independent contractor with majority of his free time collecting aircraft memorabilia with ejection seats being the main collection.

KEITH SNYDER,

born, reared and always will be a Texan. Interest in aviation grew from his father, who flew the bomber version of the F-101 out of Bentwaters, before going on to American Airlines to amass more hours in the 727 than any other flier.

Keith started photographing military aircraft in the very early 1980s, gravitating towards the Phantom because there were so many of them in Texas at the time. Met up with Bill Spidle and assisted him with *Smoke Trails* and putting together PhanCons for a few years. Served as contributing photographer for *The Hook* during the late 1980s and early 1990s.

Computer engineer by trade, Keith is married and has one daughter.

DON "HAWKEYE" SPERING,

New York born and the son of an Army career man. Fortunately there were airfields nearby and his dad built airplane models for Don and brothers Ken and Jim. Growing up during their high school years they amassed a collection of over 1,300 scale models. Designed AIR (Aircraft In Review) decals and started writing about aircraft.

His boyhood dream was to fly in a T-33 Jet. But that had to wait, the USAF gave Don his first ride in a F-106B in 1972. That started the interest in flying and photographing aircraft in the air.

During 1960 to 1985 Don worked as an administrator in the field of mental retardation, police officer and aircraft painter at McGuire AFB. Don has flown in F-100s to F-15s, A-3s to F-18s, has trapped on carriers four times and accumulated over 2,000 hours jet time. The F-105 Thud was his first true aviation love followed by the Phantom. He had 130 hours in the Phantom's backseat with cameras in hand and photographed over 300 F-4s air-to-air.

On the 35th anniversary of the Phantom, Don and friends (The Phantom Painters) painted an RF-4C Recce from Birmingham, AL unit and flew a four ship to McDonnell-Douglas plant in Missouri for the occasion where he was presented with a 100 hour plus certificate.

He has co-authored a few aviation books, written hundreds of articles and maintains a photographic stock of over 150M slides and close to a 100M black and white negatives. He is one of the original three members to start the Phantom Society. His photos appear in numerous aviation publications throughout the world, on model box tops and subjects for decals.

Don's interest in aviation continues in many aspects. He owns and operates AIR Hobby Shop and Aviation Art Gallery that specializes in unique framing and matting, AIR patches and collects and rebuilds ejection seats as a hobby along with hundreds of factory desktop models.

CLAUS JURGEN "JOSCHI" STEPHAN, born Sept. 17, 1969 in Frankfurt/M., Germany. Entered the German Air Force October 1989. Attended pilot training ENJJPT, Sheppard AFB, TX, September 1991-October 1992 and F-4 training, B-Course

BABA, Holloman AFB, NM, December 1992-June 1993.

Served with FW-71 "Richtohofen", 2nd Sqdn., Wittmund/Germany June 1993-February 1999, F-4F.

Married, he is a captain, instructor pilot T-3F, ENJJPT Sheppard AFB, TX.

WILLIAM L. SWISHER, born in Los Angeles, CA and turned 80 on Nov. 3, 1999.

With his great-grandfather in 1928 he attended the National Air Races at Mines Field. He saw the "Three Sea Hawks" (Tomlinson, Davis and Storrs) in Boeing F2B-1s (2-B-1, 2-B-2 and 2-B-3) compete with Army team, the "Three Muscateers" (J.J. Williams, J.A. Woodring and W.L. Cornelius) in their Boeing PW-9s of 95th Pursuit Sqdn. After the fatal crash of J.J. Williams, he saw Charles Lindberg fly in his place.

While attending Hollywood High School in 1936 he obtained a 616 Kodak (2-1/2 x 4-1/4 negs) as well as a driver's license and got into airplane photography in a big way. The Golden Age in southern California was a wonderful time when amateurs like Bill Swisher could get very close up and personal to famous aviators and also photograph their airplanes, such as Lockheed Electra 10EX-16020 (Amelia Earhart), Hughes H-1 NR-258Y (Howard Hughes), Douglas DC-1 NC-223Y (Howard Hughes), Lockheed 14G-102 NX-18973 (Howard Hughes), Wedell Williams NR-61Y (Roscoe Turner), Seversky AP-7 NX-1384 (Alexander de Seversky and Jacqueline Cochran), GB 7-11 NR-2101 (Cecil Allen), Howard DGA-6 NR-273Y "Mr. Mulligan" (Benny Howard), Keith Rider R-1 R-14215 (Earl Ortman), Lockheed Vega 5B NR-105W "Winnie Mae" (Wiley Post) and others.

A very big event occurred May 1937 when Gen. Hap Arnold held the GHQ AF maneuvers in southern California bringing in Army airplanes from Selfridge Field, Langley Field, Mitchel Field, Barksdale Field, as well as Hamilton Field and March Field. He was able to photograph P-26As from the 20th PG, 17th PS, 94th PS and PB-2As from the 27th PS, 33rd PS and 35th PS as well as B-10Bs from the 5th PBS, 30th BS, 32nd BS and 7th BG and B-12s from the 9th BS and 11th BS as well as B-17s from the 8th Atk. S. and 13th Atk. S.

A singular photo event of 1939 occurred Dec. 14, 1939 when at the semester end and on the return trip from Berkeley to Hollywood, he encountered 18 yellow tailed SB2U-1 and SB2U-2 aircraft of VB-2 (Lexington AG) landing at noon at Bakersfield, CA along with six red tailed BT-1s from VB-5 (Yorktown AG). This was a very rare photo opportunity considering the security restrictions that existed at that point in time. Also during that period he traded 616 size negatives with W.T. Larkin, Oakland, CA; Gordon S Williams, Seattle, WA; Donald F. Kauer, Brooklyn, NY; Peter M. Bowers, Oakland, CA and others.

Called to active duty at Fort Benning, GA Jan. 20, 1942 and was assigned as an instructor in the academic department of the Infantry School (Rife Platoon Committee) and promoted to captain March 1, 1943. He was reassigned to the 42nd Inf. (Rainbow) Div. from July 24, 1943 to Feb. 26, 1944 serving as commander of Co. G, 222nd Inf. Regt. at Camp Gruber, Muskogee, OK. He left for England as a replacement officer with the MOS 1542 (Rifle Co. commander) Feb. 26, 1944 with the invasion of France in the offing. Arriving at HQ 1st Army in Bristol, England April 15, 1944, he was assigned to the G-3 section of HQ 1st Army, Gen. Omar N. Bradley, commanding. On May 1, 1944 he was placed on detached service to the 405th FG (P-47D aircraft), 9th AF as army liaison officer stationed at Christchurch on the coast of southern England. On June 2, 1944, four days prior to D-day, he was given a top secret classification Bigot briefing on operation Overlord at Uxbridge near London. This briefing was restricted to 19 ALO officers only. On July 6, 1944 (D plus 30) at low tide he landed from a small barge on Omaha Beach at the same place that Tom Hanks did in the film *Saving Private Ryan* and then proceeded in his jeep to ALG A-8 at Picauville, Normandy to rejoin the 405th FG. His ALO job involved briefing and interrogating each mission and reporting to Army HQ any enemy information of tactical value by telephone. He also maintained the situation map showing the latest German positions with intelligence information delivered by L-5 courier planes at first light each day. Following operation Cobra and the breakout from Normandy, the 405th FG provided column cover for the 4th Armored Div. which was the lead division of Gen. G.S. Patton's 3rd Army. This continued all the way across France at close to 20 miles per day. The 205th FB was awarded a Distinguished Unit Citation for this outstanding performance during this period. From Sept. 13, 1944 to Feb. 4, 1945 he was at ALG A-64, St. Dizier, France assigned to the G-3 Section, 3rd Army. From Feb. 6, 1945 to April 22, 1945 he was at ALG Y-32 Ophoven, Belgium assigned to G-3 Section, 9th Army. From April 22, 1945 to May 8, 1945 (V-E Day) he was at ALG R-6 at Kitzingen, Germany. Finally from May 9, 1945 to June 5, 1945 he was at ALG R-68 at Straubing, Germany. While in France, Belgium and Germany he was able to photograph 32 RAF aircraft types, 91 USAAF aircraft types and 93 Germany types all in different marking schemes on 616 film during the period June 1944 to June 1945. he was relieved from active duty at Fort McArthur Dec. 19, 1945.

His civilian employment following WWII from January 1946 to Sept. 1, 1950 was as a field representative (salesman) for the AG. Chem. Div. of Swift & Co. selling fertilizers and pesticides to vegetable farmers in the Los Angeles County area.

He served at the following locations with Swift & Co., Salinas, CA., Los Angeles, CA, Winter Haven, FL and Wasco, CA. On Sept. 1, 1960 he bought into an established agricultural chemical business in Santa Maria, CA. After 18 years, June 30, 1978 he and his partner sold out to Western Farm Services and he has been retired since.

From 1946 through 1999 he photographed primarily military aircraft consistently as opportunities were available mostly in California, Arizona and Nevada. In 1957-58 he visited NAS Sanford, NAS Miami and Tyndall AFB. In May and June, 1967 he covered 15 East Coast military bases between Homestead AFB and Andrews AFB. The most intensive activity was between 1959 and 1975. In a 10 year period between 1964-74 he covered 16 Vietnam Carrier Air Group deployments of *Enterprise, Ranger, Coral Sea, Oriskany, Bon Homme Richard, Midway* and *Ticonderoga* from NAS Alameda, a number of which involved F-4 Phantom squadrons. He made 23 trips to NAS Miramar and 25 trips to NAS North Island covering Vietnam Carrier Air Group deployments of *Constellation, Hancock* and *Kitty Hawk*. Beginning with the first YF4H-1 142259 which he photographed at Edwards AFB, he has photographed most of the Pacific Fleet Navy and Marine Corps Phantom squadrons, as well as many of the East Coast based squadrons with special emphasis on squadron markings. Starting in 1950 he used color slides in addition to 616 size black and white film.

WILLIAM M. "BILL" TATE JR.,
born Oct. 13, 1944 adjacent to "old" NAS Atlanta. Growing up in the 1950s next to the air station, he developed a lasting interest in Naval aviation. While still in high school, he joined the Navy. Poor eyesight disqualified him from flight training, but he  qualified as an RO in the EC-121J at NAS Glynco, GA. Even though he was not a pilot he was still flying.

For the next 28 years he flew in a succession of naval aircraft: SP-2H, P-3A/B/C, C-9B, E-2B/C and RH-53D. In VAW-78, where he worked closely with VF 201/202, he became a Phantom "Phreak." His most vivid memories are of the September 1985 carrier quals with CAG-20 aboard CVN-69. Besides their Hawkeyes, the group included RF-8s, KA-3s, EA-6As, A-7s and the F-4Ns all of which would never go to sea as a wing again.

He retired in 1991, the only active air crewman qualified in recips, jets and helos with 3,300 hours time and 70 deck landings.

He currently resides in Birmingham with his wife Patricia and two sons, William III and James. It was here that he met Don Spering and the "Recce Rebels" and worked on the 35th Anniversary Phantom.

JAMES E. "JET" THORNELL, LTC,
comes from a military family and was constantly on the move from birth at Bolling AFB, Washington, DC, in 1948 to his present assignment at March Air Reserve Base. His recently deceased father, Lt. Col. John F. Thornell, was a leading ace in WWII. "Jimmy Jet" began his military aviation career as an F-102 crew chief in 1969 with the California Air Guard at Ontario. In 1974 he was selected to attend the last pilot training class at Moody AFB and graduated in 1975. He went on to the 549th Tac. Air Support Sqdn. after its move to Patrick AFB, FL to train in the 0-2. He was a forward air controller for the next seven years and became a flight instructor as a 1st lieutenant in 1979. His unit, the 163rd, transitioned to F-4 Phantoms in 1982. He went to Holloman AFB for fighter lead-in summer 1982 and then on to Homestead AFB for Phantom RTU. At Homestead AFB he was assigned to the 307th Tac. Fighter Sqdn. In 1983 he returned to the California Air Guard.

For the next 11 years he flew the F-4D, F-4C, F-4E and the RF-4C. In his own words flying the F-4 was the greatest achievement and experience he ever had. "I flew the best fighter of its time, with the best pilots and WSOs in an outstanding squadron, the 196TFS." During this time he had positions as chief of maintenance, chief of safety and instructor pilot. He has flown the F-4 to Spain, Korea and Canada as part of several exercises.

Today LTC "Jimmy Jet" Thornell is the chief of plans with the 163rd ARW. His career has spanned over 30 years and several thousand flying hours.

C.L. "VAL" VALENTINE, LCDR,
USNR (RET), call sign "Coke Man/Magnet," towards the end of WWII, Val was "launched" in Durango, CO while his father was touring Europe with the 10th Mountain Div.

Val's father, a 32 year career Army soldier, had some definite career goals in mind for his son (VMI or the Point); however, Val decided that slogging in the mud like his father, was not his idea of a fun time.

While attending Arizona State at Tempe in 1961, Naval officer recruiters visited the ASU Campus. Possessing the "Right Stuff" (apologies to Tom Wolfe), Val soon found himself on his way to Pensacola as a newly designated (code 1315) member of the Navy's NAVCAD Program.

He trained at NAS Pensacola, FL; NAS

Corpus Christi, TX; NAS Beeville, TX; NAS Kingsville, TX; NAS Miramar (Fightertown, USA); E'N'E School (Fairchild) and Snake School.

Units served with: VF-124, F-8 RAG; VF-111, F-8C/Ds, CAG 11 USS *Kitty Hawk*; VF-121, F-4 RAG; VF-213, F-4B/Gs, CAG 11 USS *Kitty Hawk*; F-4 FLT TEST, BUWEPSREPST Louis; VF-114, F-4J/Ss, CVW 11 USS *Kitty Hawk*.

Memorable assignments and events: Aerobatics in the T-34B and T-28-B/C (No Gs in the T-28). Car-qualing on the USS *Antietam* in a T-28C while "The Lex" was inport for major repairs. First military jet flight, Grumman TF-9J Cougar. Going plus one, Grumman F-11F-2 Tiger and realizing that Westinghouse really does mean "wasting gas." Flying the LTV F-8 C/D Crusader (Yeehaw) "When you're out of F-8s, you're out of fighters." Flying the F-4 Phantom II aka (Rhino) plus two and watching the windscreen overheat light come on! Going plus one below sea level! (Death Valley) "When you're out of F-8s, you're lucky." Fam Hops in the F-14 (1980, aluminum overcast) and the F/A-18 (1985).

Awarded DFC, Purple Heart, nine Air Medals, Vietnam Service Medal, Vietnam Expeditionary Award and Caterpillar Club, two-time member.

Currently he is a senior engineering, Corporate Programs, engineering United Airlines, San Francisco, CA.

Happily divorced, he had a daughter, Traci (deceased).

AKIRA WATANABE, born in Kawasaki, Japan in 1950 and moved to Meguro Tokyo in 1956. He used to build plastic models of military aircraft during his middle and high school days. He bought his first camera, a Canon FX in 1965 and began with airliner photography at the beginning by using black and white films. He used to go to the US airbases near Tokyo, Yokota (PACAF) and Atsugi (USN) quite frequently during 1968-72.

During that period, he took a lot of taxiing and approaching shots of F-4Cs of 347th TFW (tailcodes GG/GL/GR) based at Yokota and other PACAF Phantoms flown to Yokota including the ones with tailcodes UD/UP/UK/UE (Misawa), ZZ/ZG (Kadena), XT/XC/XN (Camranh Bay) and SA/SB/ZE/ED (TDY Kunsan). During the 1970s he took photos of USN and USMC Phantoms at Atsugi including various F-4s from the USS *Midway* and the MiG killing F-4J (VF-96/NG-100/155800). This VF-96s F-4J is his most memorable photograph taken Oct. 10, 1970 because the VG-96 pilots Cunningham and Driscoll became the aces on this plane in 1972.

He switched to use Kodachrome II/25 films instead of black and white in 1973 and started exchanging slides with foreign photographers at the same time. He visited NAS Miramar and Luke AFB in 1975 and took hundreds of F-4 shots on the flight line. He wrote and published an English written 200 page book titled *Japanese Air Arms 1952-1984* in 1984. He had lived in Torrance, CA between 1990-94 and moved again to the US, Tennessee in 1996.

Currently he lives just outside of Nashville, TN working for automotive parts (wiring harness) supplier for Nissan plant in Tennessee. His main interest is still taking photos of military aircraft and trading slides of them. He recently started flying training of glider in Tennessee and made his first solo in November 1998.

CHARLES JOHN "CJ" WEISS, took a long while to bubble to the top, but LTC CJ finally made it after 20 years in service, he stepped up to a "manly" aircraft, the F-4F Phantom II.

As an Annapolis Midshipman CJ was exposed to the lure of the legend. But it wasn't time, as after USNA graduation in 1976 and Naval Aviator Wings in 1977, he became an A-7E Fleet Carrier pilot. Lemoore Ops and cruises on the USS *American* and USS *Ranger* allowed airborne encounters with Marine and USAF Phantoms. Sentences instructing in TA-4s at Kingsville and AT-38s at Holloman provided shoulder rubbing with Marine and USAF Phantom jockeys. The pangs grew but were not to be satisfied.

CJ moved on as a combat ready F-16A pilot at Hill and at Torrejon in the F-16C. Red Flag and other large force missions meant sharing the skies with Weasels and Recces, the hunger increased. By good fortune CJ became the USAF advisor to Fort Wayne as they traded their cherished F-4Es for Vipers. The "force" is strong at Fort Wayne, the lure intensified. But satisfaction looked dim, no more US F-4s. CJ hung up his speed slacks and contributed by teaching the basics at Sheppard in the T-37. Finally a light, The USAF needed fighter guys to instruct air-to-air to new Luftwaffe Phantom aircrew at Holloman! An old guy with 5,000 plus hours was okay for them. With dust off the G-suit the "force" is finally strong with CJ. Society member No. 2194 daily passes the flame to new German aircrew. The F-4F Phantom II menace is alive and strong in our USA southwestern skies.

GAYLE WHEELER, comes from Patriot, IN. He served in the US Army working in ordnance from 1966-72. After active duty he went to Cummins Engine Co. where he works as a mechanical engineering technician. Working and talking with people who had flown or worked on the F-4 both on active duty and in the Air Guard rekindled his interest in the F-4. He became a member of the "F-4 Phantom II Society" in 1988. He is fortunate to live in the ingress and egress low level corridor to the gunnery and bombing range at Jefferson Proving Ground near Madison, IN. Seeing the F-4 fly over several times daily was a common occurrence and a delight during the 1980s and early 1990s. He likes to read any material pertaining to or about the F-4.

INDEX

The biographies are not included in this index since they appear in alphabetical order in their respective section.

— A —

Andrews AFB, MD 18, 31, 34
Andrews, Mike 39

— B —

Barnes, Ben 18
Basso, C.W. 24, 58, 75
Baxley, Capt 38
Birmingham ANG Base, AL 65, 72
Botaro, Sergio 37
Brown, Jim 2
Bruder, A. 6

— C —

Capoglu, Soner 40, 46
Causey, Capt. 38
F8U-3 Crusader III 12

— D —

Dailey, Jed 37
Daniels, R. 63
Davis-Monthan AFB, AZ 37, 67, 71, 79
Duggan, Terry 18
Duncan, Capt. 31

— E —

Edwards Air Force Base, CA 15, 50
EF-4B 13
EF-4D 13
Eisner, Steve 9
Elgin AFB 21

— F —

F-104 Starfighter 21, 22
F-105G 25
F-105G Thunderchief 14
F-110A 12, 25
F-111 19
F-14 30
F-15 Eagle 21, 22, 25
F-16 14, 21, 25
F-16 Falcon 25
F-18 Hornet 25
F-18A/B 22
F-4 Phantom 12, 31, 32, 34, 35, 36
F-46 17
F-4A 12
F-4B 12, 13, 14, 18, 19, 21, 25
F-4C Phantom 12, 13, 22, 25, 32, 37
F-4D 13, 14, 21, 22, 25, 27
F-4E Phantom 13, 14, 15, 17, 19, 20, 21, 22, 25, 31, 35, 50
F-4EJ Phantom 13, 14, 21, 22
F-4F Phantom 13, 14, 15, 17, 19, 20, 25

F-4G Wild Weasel 13, 19, 25
F-4J 13, 14, 17, 19, 25, 30
F-4J Black Bunny 14
F-4J Phantom 11, 23
F-4J(UK) 14
F-4K 14
F-4M 14
F-4N 13, 18, 19, 25
F-4S 14, 18, 19, 25
F-5A/B 22
F-8 32
F3H Demon 12
F4E 35, 50
F4G Buno 17
F4H-1 12, 13
F4H-1F 12
Fienstein, Jeffery 38

— G —

George AFB 17
Grand, Capt. 38

— H —

Hall, Mike 17, 38, 46, 57
Hamblin, Roland D. 36
Head, Michael 71
Holloway, Mike 16, 38, 65, 72
Hrapunov, Alex 31
Hughes, Dennis 17

— I —

IAI Kurnass 2000 12
Isham, Marty 22

— J —

Jacobs, Jan 9
Jay, Don 14, 15, 17
Jenkins, D.R. 15
Johnson, Wayne 30, 31

— K —

Kelly, Bill 30
Kelly, Bob 30
Knowles, Ben 37
Korat RTAFB 29
Kuntz, D.R. 17, 50
Kurnass 2000 21, 22

— L —

Lahlum, Capt. 31
Langley, R.G. 2, 39, 48, 62, 75
Larsen 29
Little, Robert C. 12
Loreille, Daniel 22

— M —

MacSorely, Frank 11
Maher, Capt. 31
Maple Flag 67, 76
March AFB, CA 5
Martin, Patrick 8, 9, 55, 67, 71, 76

Mayer, Charles 77
MCAS Beaufort 11
MCAS El Toro 30
McChord AFB 19
McClung, L.K. 62
McConnell AFB, KS 27
McConnell, Glen R. 36
McGuire AFB, NJ 34, 70
Mills, Pelham 30
Moggridge, Clive 42
Muse, Greg 16

— N —

NAF Atsugi 47
Nakane, Kikuo 21
NAS Miramar 42
NAS New Orleans 66
Naval Air Test Center 25
Nellis AFB 22
Nevada Air National Guard 75
North Dakota ANG 74

— O —

Ogawa, Masanori 22

— P —

Pacific Missile Test Center 30
Pardo, Bob 'Push' 38
Petersen, George 32, 33
Phantom CR.12-57 38
Phantom F.3 14
Phantom FG.1 23, 38
Phantom FGR.2 23
Phantom II 12
Point Mugu NAS, CA 30
PTC F-14 30

— Q —

QF-4B 13, 18
QF-4E 13, 17
QF-4G 13, 14
QF-4N 18, 25
QF-4S 25
QRF-4C 13
Quinones, Ed 18

— R —

RAAF Amberely 19
RAF Brawdy 38
RAF Fairford 71
RAF Leuchars 36
RAF Wattisham 23, 36
RAF Wildenrath 20
Ramstein AB, Germany 17
Remington, Douglas 19
Renschen, James 38
RF-101 Voodoo 12, 25
RF-104G 19
RF-4B 13, 25
RF-4C 2, 12, 13, 16, 17, 21, 22, 25, 36
RF-4E 13, 19, 20, 21, 22, 23

RF-4EJ 13, 14, 22
RF4C-Nevada Air National Guard - The High Rollers 2
Ritchie, Steve 38
RNAS Yeovilton 36
Rodriguez, Alex, Jr. 14, 15, 17
Rogers, Steve 18
Ruth, Howard B. 36

— S —

Sabato, Steven 18
Schroder, Hans 12, 74
Shepherd, Elaine 31
Smith, Wayne 25, 35, 50
Soulaine, Daniel 77
Spering, Don 2, 5, 15, 18, 27, 32, 34, 36, 37, 38, 60, 66, 70, 79
St. Louis Phantoms 60
Super Phantom 21

— T —

Tiger Squadron 15
Towle, Lt. 31
Tucker, Donny 32
Tyndall AFB, FL 17, 70

— U —

Udorn RTAFB 13, 14
USAF F-110A 12
USS Kitty Hawk 8, 17, 66

— V —

Valentine, Val 8, 17, 31, 32, 66
Van Leuven, Ken 32
Victor Whiskey 03 31
VMFA-314 30
VX-4 14

— W —

Waddington, Terry 42
Watanabe, Akira 17, 47, 51, 59, 69
Weiss, Charles 43
Wescott, Steve 18
Wilcox, Steve 44, 70

— X —

XF4H-1 12

— Y —

Yarolem, Wayne 32
YF-4J 13
YF-4K 14
YF-4M 14
YF4H-1 12
Yokota Air Base, Japan 51, 59, 69
YRF-110A 12

95

www.ingramcontent.com/pod-product-compliance
Lightning Source LLC
Chambersburg PA
CBHW081024240426
43671CB00029B/2936